To Sally,
Hope you really
enjoy this book,

♡ Patricia ✕

Also by Patricia O'Neill

Children of the Stars

Adventures
with
Angels

My Encounters with Heaven's Messengers

PATRICIA O'NEILL

Dedication

To Kevin, Ali, Victoria, and Claudia, with all of my love.

Contents

Part Two

Your Story: How to Connect with Your Angels

Part Three

Angels & Astrology

Introduction

Being the adventurous type, I have given my Angels more grief than anybody else I know. I jump into life—sometimes foolishly—and have gotten myself into some sticky situations, which, in retrospect, made me question my sanity. Yet, at the back of my mind, I have always felt safe knowing the Angels would bale me out…and surely enough, they always did! They rescued me at birth when I arrived dangerously premature and "no bigger than a sparrow," and they have saved my life countless times ever since.

Together we have hitchhiked around Europe, slept on 4th class trains in Morocco, worked on kibbutzim in Israel, taken the late metros in Paris, driven on killer icy roads in Northern Alberta, survived burst tires, bears, rapists, robbers, and the list goes on… Thanks to my winged wonder pals though, I'm still standing. It's true to say my thirst for adventure has kept them on their toes…or rather wings!

Even though some of the adventures in this book happened more than three decades ago, I remember each one as clearly as yesterday, simply because I knew in my heart that were it not for Divine Intervention at the time, I would not be alive today. In moments of despair, I relive some of these perilous moments. I find it a soothing reminder that none of us are ever truly alone, and that even in life's darkest moment, the Angels are always by our sides, ready to help in the whisper of a breeze.

Not all the stories in this book are action-packed adventures. Some are simple miracles I experienced which reinforced my belief in Angels. Other divine experiences are still perplexing to me, and are left open for your own interpretation.

I hope you enjoy this book which has been an honour for me to write, and that you, too, will experience the magic of your own personal Divine Intervention.

One Miraculous Medal

When I was seven years old, I experienced my first "Angel Aha!" moment. It was without doubt my moment of epiphany, after which I never for a second doubted the existence of Angels, or the power of prayer. It had a profound effect on me, and marked the beginning of my lifelong belief in Angels.

The year was 1964 and I was preparing in earnest for my First Holy Communion. Growing up in a staunchly Catholic Ireland, this was a major milestone in a child's life. The nuns had scared the living daylights out of us children, for fear we would forget to confess a sin to the priest during our First Confession, or not fast for long enough before receiving the blessed sacrament, or, even worse, drop the host if our tongue wasn't sticking out far enough. On no account were we to touch the host with our hands. There were so many things to remember, and I was only seven, and full of anxiety about the whole affair.

I know I should have been concentrating on the spiritual business at hand, but try as I might, all I could think about was the big white frilly dress I would be wearing, the shiny patent shoes, and the grown-up handbag, which would be filled with money gifts from all the aunties and uncles. And, of course,

1

there was the coloured jelly and ice cream the nuns were going to serve us after the ceremony.

Already, I was shaping up to be quite the little bridezilla. I worried endlessly about my veil. What if it fell off? (And it did!) I wasn't crazy about my shoes either. It would have been better if they were white, and not hand-me-downs. What if I forgot to tell the priest one of my sins during the First Confession? Would the host jump from my mouth? I'd heard some wild story about that happening to some unfortunate child, and it frightened the life out of me.

As my Communion day drew closer, I remember growing more and more anxious. I had the heirloom dress, shoes, bag, and veil, but there was one very important item missing—the Holy Communion medal. I didn't have one, and I felt it would be an absolute disaster not to have a lovely shiny medal dangling down my chest, just like every other child on the altar. Imagine an Olympian athlete standing on the podium without the big medallion—that was just how disastrous the situation was going to be without my symbolic medal. I'd stand out a mile in the class photo, or so I fretted.

The nuns taught us that in time of need, we should pray to our Guardian Angels as they answered prayers, and were there to help us. So that's who I prayed to earnestly each night. I told them I needed a medal and could they please help me to get one in time for the big day?

Days passed and still no talk of the medal. My parents were both very hard-working people, and shopping for a medal would mean a trip to the nearest big town. I didn't want to put them under pressure, either for time or for money, so I never mentioned a thing.

Shortly before my Communion day, I was running up to the church for the First Confession rehearsal. I tripped on a stone and fell with a big loud thud to the ground. Thankfully, I only grazed my knees, and as I sat on the ground cleaning the grit from my knees and clothes, my attention was drawn to a shiny object protruding between two small stones with some grass around it. Naturally, I was curious. With my fingers I began to dig around it until finally I released this mysterious shiny object. At first I thought it might be a half crown; it was the same size as one. I couldn't believe my good luck! A half crown was worth two shillings and six pence back then. I could buy a lot of sweets and treats with that.

As I held the object in my hand and began to clean the dirt from it, I was shocked to discover that it was not the customary horse image on the half crown I was gazing at, but rather the image of the Sacred Heart of Jesus on one side, and the Sacred Host on the other. What? Could this be for real? I had in fact *found* a Holy Communion medal! Nobody would believe me. I sat there looking at it in complete disbelief. My heart was literally pounding because I knew in my heart that what I had just experienced was nothing short of a miracle. What are the odds of finding a Holy Communion medal shortly before one's Communion?

What if I had never fallen in the first place? What if I had never prayed to my Guardian Angels for one? It looked like somebody had just planted it there, and was waiting for me to fall in that exact spot. But who could that mysterious person be? Nobody but the Angels knew I was praying to get a medal in time for my First Communion.

Some twenty years later, I lost the medal, along with my mother's Holy Communion medal that I wore on the same chain. Later, in anguish, I returned to the Dandelion Market in Dublin, where I felt I may have lost them, but alas! No luck. I cried and cried until there were no tears left. In the midst of my sobs, I could hear a little voice whisper in my ear, "My child, somebody else needs it now." My beloved Holy Communion medal had returned to the source, mission accomplished! Though I did feel guilty about losing Mother's medal, I took comfort in the knowledge that the medals had gone to a good home. It was somebody else's turn now to be the beneficiary of some Angel magic!

A Strange Encounter

At nineteen, I was fearless, independent, and far too cocky. (I guess that comes with being born in the Chinese year of the Rooster!) I believed the world was my oyster, and that strangers were friends I had yet to meet… Yes, I was naive. It was the 1970s in Ireland and the times they were a changin'. The land of Saints and Scholars was becoming a groovy place with the Afro hairstyles, bell-bottomed trousers, and Bob Dylan kicking up a storm!

Hitchhiking, or "thumbing," as we cool dudes called it, was the cheapest and most exciting way to travel, especially at a time when public transport was not readily available in rural towns, and I didn't have a lot of spare change in the back pocket. Besides, it was a great way to meet people, and more often than not, a lot of fun.

One balmy summer's evening, I was hitchhiking alone from Dublin to my home in the west of Ireland. Normally, this is a journey that would take up to six hours in a bus or 4-5 hours by car. It was later than usual when I eventually got out on to the road. I had stopped off in town to get some Bewley's cakes to bring home to the family. And of course the shops were so exciting, I could not resist… So between the jigs and the reels, it was getting late, and I should have known better!

Luck was on my side initially and I had no difficulty securing good speedy rides all the way down to Clare. However, by the time I got to Ennis (a town about an hour or so from my hometown), it was past 11 and by now almost dark. I had some 38 lonely miles yet to conquer. It's true to say the final leg of the journey is often the longest.

As I stood on the outskirts of the town, a swish black sports car slithered up to the kerb in a reptilian-like manner, and the man driving it rolled down the window of his car and offered me a ride. There was something about his facial expression that gave me the chills. Immediately, my Angels kicked into action and a voice in my head warned, "No! *Do not* get in that car." It was an order from Heaven! Of that I was sure.

I told the man in the black car that I was waiting for a friend to come along and that he should be here any moment. How did I think of this smart answer so quickly? I was pleased at my self-control. The driver looked irate and then sped off at a terrible pace. Some five minutes later he drove by me again, back into town this time. So if he was not even going in my direction in the first place, where exactly was he going? I knew I had a lucky escape there!

Shortly after this incident, a more cautiously driven car pulled up politely by the kerb. The driver was a man who looked in his early 40s. He rolled down his window and offered me a ride. Since he looked pretty "normal," I thanked him and hopped in. After all, there were no whispers from Heaven telling me to do otherwise!

The driver, with his hooded eyes and quiet intensity, was a man of few words. I didn't know if he was sad, or just darn strange. Try as I might to get some conversation going, he would simply nod his head, as if his tongue had been mutilated. "Do you live around here?" I ventured for the umpteenth time, really making an effort to speed up the journey, which was going about as fast as a ride on an ass and cart—and a tired ass at that! "Yes," he replied to my question, before silence fell once more like a boulder on the car.

He could be a Jack the Ripper type, I thought fearfully, sneaking a side glimpse over at him. I didn't want to stare in case he thought I was interested in him. The countryside was dotted with BFLAs (bachelor farmers living alone) in rural farmhouses, and no doubt ravenous for love. My heart began to sprint. If he was a desperate BFLA, I sure was easy prey—far too easy. Sweet Jesus, get me out of here, I remember thinking to myself. In fact, I would have preferred to be sitting on a butt-freezing donkey and cart rather than beside this peculiar man. When I recall this incident, I can see how hitchhiking was a form of insanity. We were two strangers driving together in total silence, with nothing but darkness all around us. Anything could happen!

As if hearing my thoughts, the stranger turned off the ignition in his car—rather abruptly for my liking—and in doing so, nearly stopped my heart. I knew that nothing but the power of God and the Angels would get me out of this bizarre situation unharmed!

He looked at me silently, giving the fear in me time to reach petrification level. Mr. Wacky then calmly explained that he lived up the side road that was on our left. And if I didn't mind, he would have to drop me off now. *Didn't mind?* Was he insane? He was going to literally dump me in the middle of nowhere. It was late, the whole world was asleep, and there was not a light in sight, save for the stars twinkling in the night sky. A gentleman at this hour of the night would have at least driven me to the nearest town! In hindsight, I was hugely relieved. It could have been a lot worse. At least I got out of his car unharmed.

As my not-so-knightly knight rattled away up the dirt road, leaving a trail of dust like a snail's slimy residue, I found myself standing like Mary Poppins in the middle of the road, holding in one hand the two cakes which were to blame for the whole situation I found myself in, and in the other my weekend bag. I was feeling mighty stupid, and scared at the daunting journey ahead of me. There was nothing for it but to keep on walking; at least it made me feel as if I was getting somewhere. I knew I was a good few miles from the nearest town, but my survival instinct was pretty strong—I could do this.

After a while, however, the darkness and eerie silence got to me. Would I ever get home? I thought. Where were all the cars? What would my parents be thinking? Why hadn't I brought something warmer to wear? Despair was a dangerous pit I did not want to fall into, yet I was perilously close to the edge.

Several times I looked behind me as I felt there was someone following me, yet when I looked around, all I could see was the same bleak darkness that faced me. I began to pray in earnest to my Angels and asked them to guard and protect me, and to please get me home safely!

You can imagine my utter and total amazement when suddenly, out of the blue, a soft-spoken male voice came from behind me and asked, "Where are you going, miss?" WHAT? I thought to myself, as I turned around in total shock. This journey was turning out to be an absolute nightmare of a trip. Please, Angels, where are you? I beseeched under my breath, as my heart began to explode inside my chest.

The little man was only up to my shoulders, yet I was terrified of him. I was afraid he was going to hurt me, and out here in the middle of nowhere he could do anything and nobody would know. I'd read enough horror stories in the newspapers about such things. If only my mother could see me now!

Where had he come from? I wondered, since there were no side roads nearby, and no houses within view. He came from nowhere and that is what perplexed me even more. I had heard no footsteps, and certainly did not see anybody when I had looked behind me.

I began to quicken my pace, almost running now. I told him the same story that I had told the reptilian-like man in the black car, that I was waiting for somebody to pick me up, and that he should be here any minute now. As I sped up my pace, the little man did too, continuing all the while to chat. He had a really peculiar voice and appearance. If I had to describe him in one word, it would be "leprechaun." He had a soft round face with thin hair, and was as wide as he was tall. A white aura surrounded him. He seemed to keep his distance as he walked on the side of the ditch, not getting too close to me, yet close enough to chat.

I can recall him asking me a lot of simple questions such as, "What is your name?" and "Where are you from?" With every question, a feeling of utter calm wrapped itself around me like a soothing blanket. As I looked into his kindly eyes, I knew I was safe with him, and I began to relax. As we chatted, a car passed us by—it slowed down but didn't stop. I could have sworn it was the man who gave me the ride earlier! Walking with my "lucky leprechaun" could very well have saved me a lot of trouble that night. Shortly afterwards, another car came along and this time stopped to offer us a lift. It never rains but it pours! This man had brought me luck, I thought to myself happily.

When I got into the car, I looked around for the little man, but he was nowhere to be seen. He had vanished into the thin air from whence he came! I didn't say a word as I was so shocked, and frozen to the bone. Everything felt surreal and I was exhausted. Even though it is more than 30 years since this incident happened, I never could forget my "strange encounter." I have absolutely no doubt that this little man was an Angel sent to protect me. The driver who brought me home that night was also another gentleman—I swear he must have been an Angel too!

Panic on a Paris Metro

When you mention the word *Paris*, I'll bet it brings a smile to your face as images of romance, fashion, and beauty begin to dance inside your head. This popular playground with its plethora of pleasures is a destination city for travellers young and old, and has been for time immemorial. A year in Paris is every young girl's dream, and I was no exception. It was a rite of passage I could not miss—not for all the tea in China!

When I boarded that plane for Paris all those years ago, I was truly an innocent Irish Colleen, and, like the fields of Ireland, forty shades of green. My biggest fear was having to eat raw meat, snails, and frog legs, as well as repelling advances from amorous Gallic men with their garlicky breath. Apart from a brief trip to Glasgow with my family, this was my first time *really* being away from home. It was also my first time on an airplane, so it made my destination feel all the more exotic and mysterious.

As the plane began its descent into Paris, I glanced in awe at the enormity of the city I was about to discover, and could not contain my excitement. I was champing at the bit, like an athlete waiting for the games to begin. Little did I know the action and

11

adventures that lay ahead of me… It was just as well my Angel pals were with me—every step of the way, every hour of the day!

The object of my trip was *of course* to learn French, or so I told my mother to cajole her into letting me go. My younger sister would be travelling with me, so it lessened the blow for her knowing we had each other for company and support when the going got tough.

When we arrived in Paris, we discovered, much to our chagrin, that our schoolgirl French was like double-dutch to the locals. It didn't amount to much, especially when trying to negotiate the amount we had to pay the taxi driver upon arrival at our destination. I had absolutely no idea what he was saying to us. In any case, I can recall putting money on my palm and telling him to take the amount we owed him. I wasn't fooling when I told you I was raw and innocent!

The taxi driver drove off with a big grin on his face, leaving my sister and I standing in a daze as the noise and mayhem of Paris surrounded us. It was a far cry from our peaceful little town in the West of Ireland, I thought to myself. We must have looked really sad and disorientated because a woman passing by smiled at us and said something in French to the tune of "Why so sad?" With that she took two ripe bananas from her shopping bag and gave us one each. It was such a kind gesture from a perfect stranger. It soon brought back the smile to our faces and served to remind us of our mission in Paris—to have fun! Yes, to have lots of fun, to expand our horizons *and* to learn French *mais oui!*

The taxi driver incident was the first of many upheavals to come. We discovered upon arrival that my sister's host family had casually gone away for the weekend, knowing she was due to arrive. They left her stranded. My host family reluctantly offered to take her in until her family had returned. So we were all off to a shaky start!

Life in Paris was no bed of roses. I did freelance babysitting around the city to earn extra money. One family I stayed with for a few months were having marital problems – and everybody knew about it! The air was always thick with tension. We lived in a small apartment with their children and the walls were paper thin. There was nowhere to escape. I had frequent headaches and found it difficult to sleep at night.

To say the children were rambunctious would be an understatement. They kept me on my toes for sure! One evening when their parents were gone out, they locked me in my bedroom and would not open the door. I needed to use the bathroom but could not get out. I cried myself to sleep and wondered how on earth I was going to get through this arduous and challenging time.

The final straw came one day when Madame was out shopping and the children were at school. I was busy making the beds when Monsieur came in behind me and made unwelcome advances to me. I was petrified.

I ran to my bedroom and locked the door behind me and prayed to my Angels once again. I asked them what I should do and the answer, loud and clear, was *Move!* Without further ado, I did just that. The agency promptly found me another family, but because it was at short notice, the pickings weren't great. This time I was placed in the home of a single mother with one little boy. She was dirt poor and her windowsill was the fridge. My bed was a mattress on the floor between her bedroom and the bathroom. Conditions were "tight" to say the least, but I did not care. Her little boy was a gem. I adored him and felt *safe*. A period of relative calm soon followed.

When our year in Paris was complete, my sister and I wanted to travel further afield. We planned to go to Israel to work on a kibbutz, and to travel around Europe and Morocco. In our free time, we did freelance babysitting around the city to help supplement our income. The language school where we attended had a dusty little administration office. The phones were constantly ringing with families looking for student babysitters. Fortunately, the secretary there liked us, and always gave us the plum jobs. Thus began my nocturnal adventures on the Paris Metro. Now this is where I *really* kept my Angels on their toes…pardon, I meant wings!

On the Paris Metro, I learned and saw everything I needed, or *didn't need* to see and learn about perverted men. They say Paris is "The City of Lights"—I would say more like *flashers*!

It was my own fault really, my own stupidity, which led to a potentially serious situation on the metro one evening.

After a late night child minding, I'd be given money to get a taxi home, but instead, I would run to catch the last metro, and so save on the taxi fare. It made for a more lucrative evening all round. One particular night, however, I wished with all my heart I had gotten a taxi instead. It was very late, and I was the last person to exit the metro. There was nobody else in sight, and I had a sick sense that trouble was afoot. As I was running down the empty, hollow hallway, grim with graffiti and the stench of urine thick in the air, I could hear voices coming towards me. Just as I neared my exit, I found myself face-to-face with three very dangerous looking men. They obviously worked on the metro, as they wore the green overalls worn by the metro staff. I suspected they were from Tunisia or Morocco, where a lot of the labourers in Paris came from.

I will never forget the way they looked at me, with their gold teeth glistening from afar, and evil very much in their eyes. On a fear scale, I would give the hitchhiking incident a 9 out of 10, and this one *definitely* a 12 out of 10!

The hair stood up on my arms and I felt very frightened. I was totally alone and these guys were about to pounce on me like a fox does his prey.

Suddenly, a voice—my Angel voice—told me to run, but not towards them; instead, I was to "go back the way you came and do not pass them." I did *exactly* as the Angel voice instructed me to do and began to run in the direction from where I had come. As I ran, the three men followed me in hot pursuit, which confirmed my worst fears. They were coming to get me, and not for pleasantries. I was in deep trouble, and boy did I know it!

My legs, though weak, ran faster than an Olympic athlete. As soon as I got back to the point where I had exited the metro, another train magically arrived at the station. This was odd, because my train was supposed to have been the last, or so I thought. A solitary Asian man of slight build exited the train.

He was dressed in grey and walked towards me. He had a strangeness about him, as if he was meant to be there for me! Without hesitation, I grabbed onto his arm and asked if I could walk with him until we exited the metro station.

He didn't say a word, but as I walked with him, an enormous sense of peace and calm enveloped me, just as it did with the "Lucky Leprechaun." The man in grey did not ask me why, what, or anything at all. Nor did he seem shocked that I had grabbed onto him like that.

The three nasty looking fellows in green literally stopped in their tracks as I walked away with the stranger. As soon as we reached the street, I thanked him, and ran all the way home without a backward glance. My heart was naturally pounding!

Looking back on that night in 1978, I have no doubt I was once again saved by an Angel!

Bullfighting in Spain

Spain is a beautiful country, renowned for its wonderful climate, interesting history, delicious paella, Sangria, and dare I say *bulls*! Alas, the bull we encountered in Spain was not of the four-legged species. No, the fellow who terrorized us was a two-legged beast. He was a bull in a man's clothing, which made him every bit as evil as the wolf in Little Red Riding Hood, and equally deceptive. My story this time could be amusing, were it not for the fact it was almost tragic, and certainly a very frightening experience at the time. Once again, though, the Angels came to our rescue!

The day in question was bright and gloriously sunny. My sister and I were hitching a ride to the ancient city of Granada. It was early and the day stretched ahead of us like a delicious meal about to be devoured. We were both in jubilant form, and looking forward to seeing Granada and meeting some nice people en-route.

As we stood on the roadside waiting for a ride, we were laughing as we recalled the crazy man we had met the previous day. He had stripped off all his clothing, down to his priestly black socks, and put his underpants on his head, while driving his car, all at the same time! A strange little fellow was he. It was my turn sitting in front and my sister kept calling out to me from the back seat, "Don't look! He's disgusting!!" Naturally, when somebody tells you not to look, guess what you do? Yes, you're right—I looked! I was educated. That's all I'll say about the matter!

It didn't take long to realize he was just an exhibitionist who meant us no harm—as long as we kept our eyes on the road. The things a girl has to endure to get a free ride, we joked. Little did we know there was worse to come! *Way* worse.

As the older sister by two years, I had made some ground rules to protect us before our hitchhiking adventures in Europe began. They were as follows:

Never accept a ride in a car with two men. It had to be a solitary driver, so that if trouble erupted, two against one was a safer bet for us.

Always wear rosary beads in full view. It acted as a crucifix before the devil, and was a sure protectant.

Whenever possible, choose a nice fancy 4-door car—preferably a BMW or Mercedes. Fussy we were!

Take turns sitting in the front seat. It was the most tiring position as the person sitting in front had to do all the talking! So every other car it was my turn to sit in front.

If you couldn't speak the person's language, at least speak English with their accent, and use hand gestures a lot. And, of course, laugh a lot.

Dress modestly so as not to give the wrong impression. No low-cut blouses or short butt-hugging skirts. We were good Irish Catholic girls, and were brought up well—not dragged up!

So there we were standing on the road, several miles from Granada, and not a car stopped for us. No, not as much as one! They passed us all right, but did not stop. After more than an hour standing on the road, we saw a young soldier walking along and stopped and asked him if he was also hitching. We told him how we had been waiting ages, and not one car had stopped for us. They had all been whizzing by. He explained to us that it was a holiday in Spain, and that on a holiday, it was compulsory for cars to stop and give soldiers a ride before anybody else. So that explained it! We noticed some soldiers on the road, and cars did stop for them.

Just as we were venting our frustration for the umpteenth time, a car slowly approached us, and actually stopped for us this time. It was a Ford 2-door car in a creamy yellow colour, with a red woollen blanket draped over the back seat. I can recall everything about that car, and the driver. Normally we would never accept a ride in a 2-door car, but on this particular day, beggars could not be choosers! We literally jumped in before he changed his mind.

The driver got out from the front seat and took our backpacks from us to put in the trunk of the car. He was a short stocky man with broad shoulders and had great physical strength as he hurled our heavy bags into the back of his car like they were rag dolls. He looked like a farm labourer, and his body was almost covered in thick black hair. Unfortunately, it was my turn to sit in the front seat. It did not take long to realize the driver had no English, and of course we had no Spanish, so we were off to a hairy start!

I tried in earnest to make conversation speaking English with a Spanish accent. It didn't really matter because before long it became clear to me that this bull of a man had other things on his mind. As his warm clammy hand plonked itself on my thigh, alarm bells roared in my head, and my heart began to pound. He kept repeating a word which sounded like "mwapa" which I later discovered meant "beautiful." I began to feel very uncomfortable as I did not want this fellow losing the run of himself... I just wanted him to get us to Granada—fast!

Without any warning, our bullish driver steered his car off the main road and down a dirt path. I sensed there was trouble afoot, and my fears were confirmed when he turned the car off and made a go for me. I jumped out as quickly as I could and screamed at my sister to get out of the car. When she tried to escape from the back seat, the man grabbed her and threw her to the ground. As he held her captive on the ground, I could hear my poor baby sister screaming "He's going to kill me...get him off me..." It was like a scene from a horror movie.

In one split second my whole body was taken over by what I can only describe now as not one, but several Angels. I was in my body, but somebody else was doing all the moving. I know it sounds strange, but there is *no way* I could have done what I did on that fateful day were it not for the Angels by my side. I was cool as a cucumber and the strength of Samson with it. An Angel voice told me to go and honk the car horn, which I did. The noise from the car was so loud that the man let go of my sister immediately. Thank God, he had not had a chance to harm her.

Next, I found myself grabbing the keys from his car ignition, and hurling them far off into the distant field. You'd swear I was a champion golfer. I don't know what made me do that! Actually, I do—it was the Angels guiding me. They're a pretty smart lot! It worked, because the bull man went crazy looking for his keys, and it gave us enough time to gather our wits about us.

The honking horn had also alerted some people in a far off house. In the distance I could see them walking towards us, as they must have sensed something was wrong. Our assailant eventually found his keys, and then, noticing the people walking down the hill, he got into his car and drove off. As the car zoomed away, the people retreated back from whence they came. Maybe they were Angels? The sight of them had really frightened him away.

Later, as we were walking along the road, we remembered that he had driven off with our backpacks still in the trunk of his car. Just as we were wondering where we could report him, what should we see but his car coming along towards us. Not again! This time he just stopped the car, threw us out our backpacks, and drove off with a smirk on his face. He sure was one strange beast of a man! Had he got his way, and were it not for the Angels coming to our rescue, I may not be writing this story now.

My sister said I saved her life that day, and that she will be forever grateful. I told her it wasn't me, it was the Angels—of that I have *no* doubt.

Moroccan Spice

Morocco was high on my bucket list of places I wanted to see. Having survived sunstroke in Spain, as well as countless other challenges, our stress muscles were now well developed. Little sis and I still had plenty of blank pages to fill in our adventure journals. Little did we know that after Spain, Morocco was a case of out of the frying pan and into the fire!

Romantic images fuelled our wanderlust: the excitement of haggling in the bazaars for treasure, inhaling aromatic spices, watching belly dancers and snake charmers, visiting atmospheric Medinas, Riads, and magical mosques, eating delicious Moroccan couscous dishes, seeing the Atlas Mountains, Casablanca, and Marrakech, sunbathing on beautiful beaches… Morocco had it all in abundance, and we wanted to see and taste every single morsel.

What we didn't realize, however, was the fact that Morocco was a dangerous place for young girls to visit. This was back in 1978 when women in Morocco had very little freedom, and foreign women travelling alone were regarded as little more than prostitutes. A day at the beach for a Moroccan woman meant sitting inside a tent, covered from head-to-toe, while her husband and children could do what they wanted. Many of the men would flirt with Westerners like us because they perceived us as "easy." No wonder my Angel pals were on guard 24/7!

In addition, I had no idea how enormous Moroccan cockroaches were! I'm sure if you were hungry enough, you could enjoy a tasty cockroach dinner. I did not like the cheeky way they crawled over your toes as you sat down for a meal. And it wasn't just the cockroaches that made my skin crawl either—the filth and stench of the back streets was just as bad.

Once, when travelling on the 4th class carriage of a train along with the toothless mountain men, near-headless chickens, smelly fruit and vegetables, and dirt poor locals, I awoke from my slumber to find a strange man's fingers wandering up my legs. No, it wasn't a cockroach this time! I felt like telling the offender that no, I wasn't a piano or a prostitute. Instead, I gave him a good whack with my bag, and thankfully that was the end of that! My Angels had to work 24/7 to keep me safe in Morocco. It was a tough grind.

Before discovering the charms of Morocco, we had to get there. So, taking our adventurous spirit and backpacks with us, we boarded the ferry in Algeciras, Spain which brought us to the city of Tangiers in Morocco. It was a short and very pleasant hop from Spain to Morocco and before we realized, we had landed! Just as we were trying to get our bearings after departing the ferry, and looking around for a bus or taxi, we were approached by two young men dressed in ankle-length white robes. One was tall and slim, while his companion was considerably shorter. They looked like they were on a mission…but what kind of mission? In a very businesslike manner, they produced their identity cards, and told us they worked for the Moroccan Tourist Board, and that their work was to show tourists like us around Tangiers. Because they seemed genuine, the fact that it sounded too good to be true never entered our innocent heads!

Without further ado, the boys hailed a fancy taxi. We told them we were looking for a good youth hostel to stay for a few nights. "Oh, we can find you a nice luxurious hotel for the same price," the older fellow said. "C'mon, we'll bring you there now." He started speaking to the taxi driver in his local tongue, which, of course, was double-dutch to us.

After a short taxi ride through congested, filthy streets, the taxi driver pulled up outside a luxurious looking hotel. The cool white marble interior of the hotel was a welcome respite from the savage Moroccan heat. "Are you sure this hotel is the same price as a youth hostel?!" I asked the older fellow, not at all convinced he was telling us the truth. "Absolutely!" he said, convincingly. I assumed he was able to get a good price for us because he worked for the tourist board. Once again, he and his friend began to speak in foreign tongues to the hotel manager, who smiled at us, displaying glittering gold teeth and a lecherous expression. Why would the Moroccan Tourist Board want to entertain penniless students like us? I asked myself, yet I was being sucked in by the comfort of it all, and really did not want to question it all too much. Besides, this was all so exciting!

The boys told us they would give us a few hours to relax and unpack, and that they would return that evening to bring us for dinner and show us around Tangiers. True to their word, they picked us up from the hotel around suppertime, and drove us to an exotic spinning restaurant. They explained that it was one of the first rotating restaurants to be built in Morocco, but that sadly the architect had died during construction. Our hosts seemed well educated and surprisingly polite. We had a lovely dinner, which was followed by traditional Moroccan entertainment— belly dancing, and dancers dancing with glasses of water on their heads. It was a wonderful evening.

After they returned us to our hotel, the boys said they would return the following day and bring us to see the famous Caves of Hercules outside the city. Not once did either fellow give me the sense they were trying to become romantically involved. I think the taller fellow liked my sister, but certainly there was no chemistry between the shorter fellow and me. But nevertheless, the two young men continued to show us around, and I was very much aware that lots of money was being spent on us. But for what purpose?

On the evening of the third day of being wined and dined, I was roused from my sleep by a loud voice telling me, "GET OUT FAST!" It wasn't a dream, but rather a message from my Angels that danger was imminent. I had become good at recognizing those voices, and knew from the message that we needed to do just that—GET OUT FAST!

I wakened my sister and told her we needed to leave the hotel. Something was not right. Just before breakfast, with our bags all packed, we went to Reception to check out. The lecherous manager who greeted us when we first arrived was there and, when we tried to settle up, informed us that the boys had supplemented our stay. We discovered that the hotel was in fact four times more expensive than the youth hostel would have been! We ended up having to pay the full whack for our last day.

So why did the boys lie to us saying it was the same price as a youth hostel when it obviously wasn't? Why did the younger fellow seem so agitated as if he was working for somebody other than the Tourist Board as he had led us to believe? Romantically speaking, he certainly wasn't working on me! If they could lie about the hotel, then surely their working for the Tourist Board of Morocco must have been one big fat white lie too!

Why did my Angels rouse me from my sleep in the middle of the night and tell me we must depart immediately? I have thought back on that experience, and believe we were being groomed to either traffic in drugs or the slave trade, which in 1978 was a burgeoning industry. One thing is for sure—my Angels had once again come to our rescue, and we got out in the nick of time!

A White Butterfly

It was one of those grim post-Christmas days in January when you break all your New Year's resolutions in one fell swoop! The dense snow outside held me captive indoors, and, like my dogs, I was suffering from a severe dose of cabin fever, which nothing in my medicine cabinet could cure. I was living in Calgary at the time, and if you know anything about Alberta winters, you'll know they are not for the faint-hearted. However, Calgary was a paradise compared to Fort McMurray in Northern Alberta, where we first landed from Ireland in November 1992. That first Christmas it was 50 degrees below with the wind chill! Cabin fever was more common than colds. By way of consolation, cold and flu bugs could not survive in the extreme cold, so we were spared that inconvenience.

It certainly would have helped if I were the sporty, outdoorsy type. Alas, I'm not. I do not like skiing, cold weather, or snow. And with good reason! I've lost track of the number of times I have slipped on the snow and ice. It is messy, and I missed not being able to wear nice heels. Those snow boots and huge padded parkas made me feel short and fat! Once, I fell so hard I banged my head off the frigid ground, and actually saw stars!

Another time during a skiing lesson, I fell and broke my ankle. I had to have surgery and was in a cast for months. So yes, I had plenty of reasons for not liking snow.

Nor did I like the dry air that caused me so many nosebleeds, and forced me to buy expensive skin creams so my skin wouldn't ache so much or look wrinkled like a dry old prune. And I detested getting electric shocks every time I touched an appliance—or worse still, when I touched cold stainless steel handles and got nasty frost burns.

On the day in question—the butterfly day—I was feeling mighty fed up and had broken one of my resolutions not to eat chocolate. I was looking out at the snow and really dreading the thought of spending the rest of my life imprisoned for several months of the year like this. And I was missing the green green grass of home.

I needed to get out of the house fast! But where to? The mall would be gloomy. Everybody was broke after Christmas. The snow was too deep to go for a drive in the car, and besides, it would be slippery and dangerous. Feelings of frustration and desolation washed over me.

I asked my Angels to let me know they were with me that day, to give me some sort of clue before I went krazee! I suggested the sight of a butterfly to console me, as butterflies are symbolic of transformation. I knew full well it was January, and with the snow still thick on the ground, a butterfly would be next to impossible to see. But not for the Angels! That wasn't nice of me to trick them like that, but I was desperate for a sign.

As soon as it stopped snowing, we managed to make our way to church for Sunday mass, and what a treat it was to be able to get out of the house. As I was walking in the door of the church, I came face-to-face with a lady wearing an enormous white butterfly brooch on her coat collar. It was so big you could not miss it! And if that was not proof enough, later on our way home I passed a building with a giant picture of a butterfly on it. Yes, my Angels were indeed with me. I saw my butterfly that day!

Feathers from Heaven

Not a day goes by that I am not in regular communication with my Angel friends—some days more than others. I can feel their presence very close to me, especially in the car when I am driving with the radio off. If I am very still, I can sometimes hear the flutter of wings. In some terrifying situations (i.e. Highway to Hell), they have taken over the steering wheel for me and given me the strength and calm I would not otherwise have had. Yes, I know my Angels are always just a hair's breadth away.

There are several methods I employ to communicate with them, and they with me. First thing in the morning I recite my Angel prayer, which goes like this:

> *"Oh Angel of God, my sweetest guardian dear*
> *To whom God's love commits me here*
> *Ever this day, please be at my side*
> *To enlighten and guard, to rule and guide."*

Next, I call upon the all-powerful Archangels (Michael, Raphael, Uriel, and Gabriel), and say a little prayer to each of them, as follows:

"Archangel Michael, I call upon your tender mercy to please keep evil thoughts, words, and actions far from my loved ones and me this day. Shield us from harm."

"Archangel Raphael, please help me to have a healthy mind in a healthy body."

"Archangel Uriel, please surround me with good friends who are loyal and true and who have my best interests at heart. Protect me from false friends."

"Archangel Gabriel, please help me to be creative in my thoughts, words, and deeds this day."

First thing in the morning when the coffee is brewing, call upon your Angel guides to protect and help you throughout the day ahead. I guarantee if you do so, you will have a far more pleasant day. When strife does knock upon your door, call upon them to help you deal with it. They are always beside you—you simply need to be silent in your thoughts to hear them speak. Remember, nothing can happen to you that you or your Angels cannot handle together! The Archangels are truly a force to be reckoned with. As you pray to them for help, you will feel immediately empowered.

If I am having a difficult day, or have some pressing question to ask the Angels, they employ different methods for giving me my answer. They always return my call without fail!

As in the story of the white butterfly, they did not let the cold January snow prevent me from seeing a butterfly that day.

This assured me they had heard my request. I also use angel cards to receive an answer to a question. I especially like Doreen Virtue's Angel cards. I ask a question to the Angels and focus on the question in my mind, while at the same time shuffling the cards. Whenever a card mysteriously jumps from my hand and on to the floor, I know that the message on that card is what they want me to read. It works!

Another welcome Angel communication comes to me through fortune cookie messages which I find in the most random of places. I have found them beneath trees, on the street, under seats, furniture, etc. Once, I even found one miraculously beneath a church pew! What are the odds of finding a fortune cookie message in a church? Whenever I ask the Angels for advice, I then have to be on the lookout for their answer, and the fortune cookie message is just one method of response.

Without fail, they respond in ways that tell me it's my Angels on the line! Feathers from heaven in odd places, messages on car bumper stickers, or passing lorries…the message I read will be very apt to the situation, and sharp as a razor.

Recently, I lost my handbag with my purse and all the contents. It was two days before I was due to travel to Ireland. I was frantic because my visa and all my cards and money were in it. It was missing a whole day and night, and along with it a good night's sleep! I had turned the house literally upside-down, and still no luck. Why do these things happen to me just before I am due to fly? I wondered to myself this particular day. I had been very busy trying to get myself organized to travel. It's never easy leaving home and organizing family and pets, etc. Naturally, I prayed my heart out to St. Anthony, who has never failed me yet! I have promised him that if ever I have a grandson, I'll persuade my daughters to put Anthony in the name! I love that saint. And, of course, I begged my beloved Angels to help me find that darned naughty bag!

Next morning as I was walking into my office, I saw this huge white feather sitting on the ground in a random place. I breathed a huge sigh of relief. I knew instantly that I would find my bag. It was their way of telling me. Sure enough, as soon as I got into my office, the bag was waiting for me under my desk, in a place I never would have put it. The cleaners had obviously put it there. And what honest cleaners they were!

Even though I wished I had been saved all this stress, I knew it was a kindly reminder from my celestial buddies that I needed to SLOW DOWN and live in the NOW! Things like that happen to me when I have departed from the moment, and am miles ahead of myself. Thank God and my Angels, there was a happy end to this story!

I could fill a hundred thousand pages with similar stories, but there are two more which come to mind, as they were indeed spectacular.

One time I was in a state of limbo as to what career I should pursue, now that my children were growing up, and starting university. My gut instinct was writing and communication, as it is my passion. Once again, I enlisted the guidance of my Angel advisors to let me know if I was on the right track. The answer came shortly afterwards…

I was walking on a beautiful beach in County Wicklow, Ireland. It was a particularly windy day and I could hardly see because the wind kept blowing my hair into my eyes, so I kept my head down, looking at the sand until the wind died down. Suddenly, my eye was drawn to a grey-coloured Parker pen standing upright in the sand—it was waiting for me! There was no way I could miss it. What struck me about the pen was the feather, which is symbolic of Angels and also of course Parker pens. In addition, the colour grey reminded me of Grey Eagle, a spirit guide I had read about in the book *The Eagle and the Rose* by Rosemary Althea. I was advised to read this book by a psychic I had gone to visit some years ago.

Not long after this pen incident, I was back home again in Canada and driving in my car one day. Suddenly, without warning, a huge grey feather got stuck in my rear view mirror. It was so big and distracting I had to stop the car to remove it. Nothing like that had ever happened to me before, but it was worthy of note. I knew the Angels were trying to tell me something.

But there was more to come…

Several days later, I was walking my beloved angel dog, Lulu, when she stopped to sniff a lamppost. As I waited patiently, allowing her to get "high," my eye was immediately drawn to a curious looking stone standing upright in the ground, in the same way the grey Parker pen stood in the sand.

I went over and pulled it from the earth. I knew in an instant this was no ordinary stone. Next day, I brought it down to the gem store in town and asked them what it was. It turned out to be a piece of rutilated quartz. I looked up the properties of rutilated quartz, and apparently it helps to channel your spiritual connections!

One day, I was driving my husband into the office. As he got out of the car on the passenger side, his leg got stuck in the straps of my handbag and it fell out of the car. The contents spilled all over the ground. Just as I was putting everything back into the bag, I found a beautiful silver ring on the ground. The stone on it also happened to be rutilated quartz. I recognized the golden strands of light in the crystal clear stone, similar to the stone I had found. It was absolutely beautiful. Not thinking anything, I was sure it must have fallen out of the car, and that it belonged to one of my daughters. It certainly was not mine. Later when I showed them the ring, they were amazed. It did not belong to any of them! Where did this mysterious ring come from? It was such a mystery. The ring fit me perfectly, and I now wear it when I write. It was meant for me.

Last, but certainly not least, was a sign that touched me deeply. I was walking in a mall one day, my mind deep in thought as to whether I should pursue a career in Real Estate, or concentrate on writing, which was my first love. Suddenly, at my feet, I found a grey eraser in the shape of an elephant on the ground. I found it particularly touching because my godmother, who died when I was six years old, always gave me little things with an elephant theme. She used to say that just like elephants, I had a retentive memory! She gave me my very first book, *The Saggy Baggy Elephant*, which I still have, and she would always give me erasers in the shape of elephants. So what are the odds of finding a grey eraser in the shape of an elephant right in the middle of a squeaky clean, marble-floored, generic shopping mall?

And if that was not ENOUGH in terms of signs, there was more to come. I was having coffee with a friend one day in Starbucks, and as we left the café, my eye was drawn to a Jones bottle top sitting on a table. I said to my friend, "Wait, I must read the message on the bottle top!" She laughed, as she thought this was very funny. But what do you think the message on the bottle said?

You have a way with words. Use it.

I still have that bottle top and keep it on my desk when I write, along with my crystal rutilated quartz stone, elephant eraser, feathers, grey Parker pen, medals and many fortune cookie messages I have found, and all sorts of other inspiring odds and ends.

Who knows? Maybe this is what I am meant to do? I certainly hope so!

Visions in White

For as long as I can remember, I have always been aware of the presence of spirits, and as I look back and reflect on these profound experiences, I have come to the conclusion that what I initially thought was a ghost may in fact have been an Angel. There have been several sightings over the years, but three incidents in particular stand out in my memory.

The first one happened around midnight on the 8th of July, 1983. It was the night before my wedding day. It was a very warm night and sleep had eluded me. There was so much on my mind, least of all the thought of all that lay ahead of me the following day. I tossed and turned and wished to God I could get a good night's sleep so I wouldn't have big black rings under my eyes on my wedding day. I didn't want to be tired and sleep deprived on the biggest day of my life.

Suddenly, my darkened bedroom became aflame with light. I could see very clearly what appeared to be a woman in a long, white dress standing beside my bed. I was so frightened I jumped under the covers, leaving just enough room to breathe. My heart was pounding with fear. Thankfully I fell asleep shortly afterwards, and did not raise my head from under the blankets!

The next morning when I awoke, all I could think of was this strange apparition. Deep in thought, my eyes were drawn to the dressing table. On it stood a little plastic statue of Our Lady. It was given to me as a wedding present by a Christian Brother who was a friend of the family. The statue was luminous. That must have been it! I said to myself with a laugh. It must have been the statue glowing in the dark! I told everybody the story of the glow-in-the-dark statue, and they thought it hilarious.

Years later, after I experienced some more apparitions, my memory went back to that incident. No, it couldn't have been the glow-in-the-dark statue, after all. What I had seen was much larger than the little 12-inch statue on my dressing table. That I know now for sure -- I have lots of glow-in-the-dark items, and they remain the same size! Besides, I had been awake for ages in the darkened bedroom, and hadn't noticed it before. What I saw was huge, and lit up the whole bedroom in an instant, not just 12 inches on the dressing table. I was thankful that my Angel friend had helped me to get to sleep!

The second incident happened in the summer of 1994 when I lived in Fort McMurray, Alberta. I was heavily pregnant at the time with my third child, Claudia. I can recall the incident very clearly. I was uncomfortable, and far too hot. There was no air conditioning in our rental home, and the heat that summer's night was unbearable.

As I lay on my side of the bed, eyes open in the pitch black bedroom, listening to my husband's gentle snoring, I contemplated getting up and doing some ironing. Whenever

I cannot sleep, that's what I usually do! I became too lazy and cozy to get up, though, so just stayed in place.

Suddenly, a large, white, smoke-like presence appeared on the wall to the right of the fireplace at the end of the bedroom. I gazed at it in surprise rather than fear. I wasn't frightened because I had Kevin in the bed beside me, and knew I could give him a dig in the ribs and wake him up if needs be.

To explain, this bedroom was always pitch black, which was an issue for me. I hate dark bedrooms, preferring a little light to stray in. The two windows on the left side of the room were covered by venetian blinds that succeeded in blocking any glimmer of light. So when I saw this white smoke appearing on the wall, my eyes were glued to it. I knew this was a presence and it had movement. What happened next actually brought tears to my eyes. The smoke-like vision cleared, and before my eyes I saw the image of huge rosary beads on the wall. It remained only for a few seconds, and then disappeared. So gentle, so moving.

I got out of bed and sat on the edge for a long time, wondering if I should wake Kevin up, and tell him what I had just seen. I decided I would wait until next morning, as it would not be fair to wake him when he had a day's work ahead of him. The first words out of my mouth the following morning were "Kevin, we need to pray the rosary morning and night!" and then I told him about the vision I had seen on the wall.

It is 20 years since this incident happened, and I still don't know what to make of it. My conclusion is that we need to pray!

The third incident, still glued to my memory, happened in my hometown of Kilkee, Co. Clare, Ireland. It was August 1996, and I was on holidays with the children. Kevin had returned to Canada weeks before us for work. We were sleeping in the mobile home located beside my parents' house. There was a big family get-together that weekend, and we were due to return to Canada early the following week.

My nephew and his friends were sleeping in a tent pitched in the grass outside the mobile home. They were talking and laughing and I could hear their voices, but not what they were saying. I was on my own and found it really difficult to sleep that night, so I tossed and turned endlessly.

Quite unexpectedly, and clear as day, an image of Our Lady's face appeared to the left corner of the sink. It was just a shoulder length image, and breathtakingly beautiful. She wore a crown on her head. The image lasted just a few seconds, but long enough for me to take it all in. As soon as the image disappeared, I turned on the light. It was just 2:00 a.m. I was so overcome with what I had just seen that I burst into tears and could not stop crying. It was such a profound experience, and one that has lingered in my memory for many years—simply because I have wondered *why?* Why did I see this remarkable image?

My gut instinct at the time was to phone Canada and tell Kevin, but it was two in the morning and I would have to go over to the house and wake my parents up. I didn't want to do it. Instead, I just prayed and killed time until morning came. Naturally, after such an experience, sleep was far from my mind!

Next morning, I told my parents what I saw, but their reaction was, I think, like most peoples' would be—a little "dubious." As soon as I was able to call Kevin I told him about my profound experience that night, and seeing the vision of Our Lady in the room. He told me that he had had a strong urge to pray that very same day! In fact, he had even gone out to a Christian store in Calgary, where we lived at the time, and bought prayer books for all the family, rosary beads for himself, and a book about reflections on Christian experience. What are the odds? As he said himself, this was quite out of character for my husband. He felt that the image I saw was that of an Angel.

Last, but certainly not least, I made the connection that the very day I saw this image—August 15—was the Annunciation of our Blessed Virgin! I am ashamed to admit I did not know it at the time, but later discovered the co-incidence of that date! These three apparitions were perplexing to me—and still are.

Highway to Hell

In the summer of 2008, I was busy getting final bits and pieces together for my first book, *Children of the Stars*. I had an appointment with my book designer one afternoon in Langford, a commuter belt town located about 30 minutes from the city of Victoria where I live (30 minutes depending on traffic and how fast you drive!).

I remember it was a Friday, and I wanted to avoid the huge rush hour traffic jam which usually began around 4 pm. Traffic on the Pat Bay Highway is always horrendous with folk rushing to get home, and I don't like highway driving at the best of times.

On the day in question, I left my office around 2:30. I had just got as far as the elevator when a fierce sense of foreboding came over me. I didn't know what it was, exactly—I just got the feeling that something was about to happen to me. Even though I was rushing to get on the road, I returned to my office and blessed myself with some holy water that I always keep on my desk. As I blessed myself, I said a little prayer to God, Our Lady, and my Angels to drive with me in the car.

(As an aside, let me tell you that I keep holy water in little bottles all around the place—you just never know when you may need it! Like the day we had a very evil man come into our office. I work with my husband, who is a psychiatrist, and we meet a variety of people from all walks of life—not to mention ex-prisoners—and on one occasion even a murderer! This very strange man came into our office one day, and I sensed a terrible, satanic, evil presence from him. After he left, Kevin came out from his office, and I could see from the look on his face that he felt the same! I had to sprinkle the water all over the place to purify the office).

After I had blessed myself with the holy water, I got into the car. I was driving my husband's car, as I had a new one I wanted him to break-in for me. (I'm usually nervous with any new machinery or gadgets, and always get Kevin to "break it in" for me. The only exception being new clothes!).

Halfway down the "Highway of Hell" as I call it, I noticed the car started to act really strange, as if it had a puncture. The tires were making quite a racket, and did not feel quite "right." I knew something was wrong. I was petrified as I gazed around at the motorists all driving like crazy. A puncture at this time would have been most inconvenient. What was I to do? There was no place where I could stop the car, so I said a little prayer and asked God and the Angels to please get me to Langford safely! I stayed cool, calm, and collected. Fortunately, I was able to get to my destination without a hitch.

As soon as I arrived, I asked my book designer, Jim, to have a look at the car, explaining what had happened to me en-route. He very carefully checked all the tyres, and then told me he couldn't see any evidence of a puncture, but suggested I bring the car into a garage upon my return to Victoria.

After we concluded our book business, I got back into the car—not without saying a prayer first for a safe journey home! Again, just when I was halfway home, the car began to suddenly jolt like crazy. I could barely handle the steering wheel this time. It was one of the most frightening experiences of my life. If I lost control of the car, I could crash into others and there would be a huge pile-up—not to mention loss of lives. "Please God, help me!" I prayed aloud. This was serious!

Suddenly, a force came over me—just like the time in Spain when my sister and I were hitchhiking and had to fight for our lives. I remember at the time feeling like a puppet with a mysterious puppeteer guiding me. It was the same now. I was sitting at the steering wheel, but somebody else was driving it for me. I know for a fact that the mysterious puppeteer was my Angel. A calm came over me, and I knew everything would turn out all right, despite the fact the noise inside the car was ferocious! There was something seriously the matter with it.

Calmly, my Angel guided me until we got off the busy motorway. The minute we turned into the slower lane, lo and behold! The front tyre rolled straight off the car. It crossed to the other side, and missed a new red Audi by seconds. That wasn't all—driving right behind me was an off-duty policeman in a big white truck. What are the odds? I had no phone with me, and I was shaking like a leaf, as was the man in the red Audi and the off-duty policeman. They had never in their lives seen such a narrow escape.

The three of us stood looking at each other in a daze. Then by the grace of God, the policeman flew into action phoning for a tow truck, and for Kevin to come and get me, and all the other bits and pieces. They pulled the offending tyre off the road, and even offered to get me a cup of tea. I tell you I surely must have friends in high places!

The first thing I did when I got out of the car was to put my hands in my pockets, just for comfort. And what do you think I found in my pocket? It was a miniature statue of Our Lady, given to me by my mother after another near-death car accident we had when I was 15. It is only a few inches high, but it had saved our lives before, so my mother gave it to me when I was coming to Canada. I always kept it on the dashboard of my car, but since I had just got a new car, I'd taken it from my old car before selling it. I intended to put it on the new vehicle, but had not got around to doing it yet. In fact, I'd even forgotten it was in my pocket! The minute I saw it, I just said, "Thank you, Our Lady."

Without doubt, it was a close call. Can you imagine the carnage that would have happened if the wheel had fallen off on that crazy busy highway? My husband had just brought the car in to have the winter tyres taken off, and the mechanic in the garage must not have put the tyre back in correctly. When the car was towed and they heard my story, they knew they too had had a close call!

The Warning

Since we are talking about automobiles, and what happens when they go out of control, I must tell you about the incident that led to my mother giving me the little broken statue of Our Lady that I keep on the dashboard of every car I drive.

It was 1972 and I was 15 at the time of my first ever automobile accident. For several weeks prior to the accident, I kept having recurring dreams about being in a car crash. In the dream—or rather, nightmare—our car had lost control, and kept turning over and over again on the road, ending upside down. In the end we all walked out alive. Why did I keep having this same weird dream? I wondered. Little did I know I was soon to find out!

When my older sister Vivien started her first job with Allied Irish Banks in Ennis, 34 miles from home, my parents, younger sister, and myself went with her "for the spin," as we say in Ireland. It was a lovely day and we were all nervous and excited for Vivien starting her first job away from home.

Somewhere on the road between the town of Kilrush and Ennis (the same road where I was hitchhiking at 19!), one of the tyres must have driven over a nail or something, because we had a blowout and the car went completely out of control.

It all happened so quickly—one minute we were all happy and laughing in the car, the next minute we were turned upside down, literally and physically!

The car started to spin out of control, and began to roll over and over on the road, ending upside down—there was that dream, enfolding before my very eyes. As the car rolled, and everybody was screaming, I remember feeling very calm. The whole situation was surreal. Even though I got a bit of glass in my eye, and had blood pouring down my face, I knew we would all be safe so I did not panic.

I could hear my mother scream some prayers, and tell us to get out of the car quickly. She was unbelievably cool, given the circumstances. The next thing I remember was her jumping out of the car, and running up the road to find the little statue of Our Lady which had fallen out of the car, and, remarkably, she found it.

Back in 1972, there were no mobile phones, which would have been so useful at a time like this. Mother was in full control of the situation however, and as cool as a cucumber, God bless her, though poor Daddy was a nervous wreck. She told my sister and I to run down the road and knock on the nearest neighbour's door for help.

Not far from the accident scene, there was a cream-coloured house situated back in a bit from the road. I am sure I must have looked pretty strange, knocking on their door with blood pouring down my face. Not as strange, however, as the residents of the house. They gave "strange" a whole new meaning! It was truly like something from a horror movie. The house was furnished with seats from old cars, and very little else. I can remember thinking how odd it looked.

There was no urgency about the fellow who answered the door to us. I think he was not the full shilling. We told him about the accident, asking if we could please use his phone to get some help, and he looked at us as if we were aliens from another planet. "Where are you from?" he kept asking over and over, and "What's your name?" I think we gave up, and went to the next house. In retrospect, one had to see the humour!

Thank God the Angels had warned me in advance! After the incident, I never had that dream again! All's well that ends well.

In the Cold Canadian Wilderness

Nothing prepared me for the frigid temperatures of Fort McMurray, Alberta. We arrived on the 15th of November, 1992, when the snow was knee high, and winter had well and truly set in—with a vengeance, I might add. Temperatures outside were nearly 50 degrees below with the wind chill—a savage climate by all accounts.

There was a sinking feeling in my heart as we walked into the desolate airport terminal. It seemed so empty and lonely, devoid of any kind of sparkle or warmth. To add to my misery, there was nobody there to greet our little family, having just made our way halfway across the world. This place was a fertile field for frustration—I could tell. We were in the middle of nowhere: 300 miles from Edmonton, and nothing in between! The few stragglers we saw around the place looked equally miserable.

Having come from Ireland, I was glammed up to the eyeballs, with my dark mink hat, orange wool coat with matching mink fur collar, and black leather gloves. I was representing my country after all, and couldn't let the side down to the Canadians! "You're wasting your sweetness on the desert air," I thought to myself. I may as well have worn my saggy baggy tracksuit and fleece jacket, for all anybody cared! Nobody seemed to bother about fashion in these parts, just comfort and warmth; it was a case of survival of the fittest. The ground in the terminal was messy and slippery from all the snow being dragged in from outside, so my high heels were a tad unstable. Yes, I was feeling mighty sorry for myself, and with good reason.

The hospital Kevin was going to work for had given us the use of a house rent-free for a few months until we found a place to rent. That was the good part! The keys to this house were left in an envelope at the Arrivals desk. As Kevin went over to the desk to collect the keys, I said a little prayer to myself: "Sweet Jesus, keep me sane!" It was short and to the point. This was going to be a tough station…and boy, during those stark early months, it surely was.

Ali was only three and a half years old, and Victoria a tiny baby eight weeks old. I was petrified they would catch a cold or frostbite, so had to bundle them up from head to toe whenever we ventured out. Somebody said you had 20 seconds before frostbite set in, so I was always working against the clock. I should have done a course in dressing for a Canadian winter before I came to Canada. It would have helped!

My vanity died a death the first day at the airport. Fashion became secondary to practicality. Big bulky parkas replaced my glam wool coats, the heels were replaced with fat sloppy snow boots, and, horror of horrors, I knew the end of civilization had come when I was forced to wear a balaclava! I thought only fellows robbing banks wore those atrocious garments. Not so. I remember it was a green-coloured one, and I hated wearing it. No way would I ever have my photo taken wearing that monstrosity! But I didn't want frostbite on my face either. There was no choice. When in Rome you have to do what the Romans do!

The winters there are very long, and people tended to stay bundled up in their homes. I stayed indoors with the children all day long, doing crafts, baking, watching television, and just having fun. There was no Facebook, and phoning Ireland was a luxury. The girls were delighted to have Mum's undivided attention, and we bonded. That was a good thing. It was too cold and dangerous to venture out, and besides, I had not got my Canadian driving licence yet. Thank God I had the children, because otherwise I would have gone berserk! Poor Kevin was run off his feet at the hospital. He was the only psychiatrist for 36,000 people. Our social life was limited, as he did not want to keep bumping into patients at parties, which was understandable.

As soon as the children were tucked cosily into bed, it was "Momma time." Television and the Sears catalogue became my bosom buddies. My job was to keep us all happy and sane, and shopping helped!

Things vastly improved once the cold snap passed, and we could get out and about for nice slushy walks in the snow. The air, though frigid, was very pure and quite pleasant. The skies were frequently a lovely turquoise blue, which contrasted nicely with the sugar-white snow. The girls loved to play snow angels and make snowmen. Despite that, I never really cared too much for snow—I found it far too messy, and disliked the fact I could never wear my nice elegant heels. With my big bulky parka and short sloppy snow boots, I felt like the Michelin Man. Besides, skiing gave me nothing but a broken leg! If I sound lacking in enthusiasm for winter sports—you got it!

As soon as I passed my driving test, it was full steam ahead. Goodbye four walls, hello world! I was so happy to be able to drive around and get to know my way around Fort McMurray—I felt like a prisoner released from prison. The shops were of a very high standard since there was so much money floating around the place, and nowhere else to spend it. Oil is the big business there, with the oil sands generating steady and lucrative employment. Then of course the employees had to be serviced by doctors, shops, etc., and soon a town was born. People flock to Fort McMurray from all over the world, and by the time my two and a half years were up, I had met a lot of very interesting and cosmopolitan people. The parties there were the best and most extravagant I have ever experienced in my life. It is jokingly called "Fort McMoney" for obvious reasons. Women are in short supply, so it's a great place to find a mate!

Before I got my licence, Kevin would have to drive me everywhere, and wait outside with the car running all the time. If you turned the engine off, the car may not start again because of the extreme cold. In those early days, we learned the hard way that cars needed to be plugged in at night, and that if you left a can of Coca Cola in your car, it too would freeze up in minutes—even if the car was in the garage!

So now I had my driver's licence, in a place where some locals would not drive their cars when the weather was that extreme, for fear of accidents. The black ice beneath the snow made for treacherous driving conditions, but who was I to know?

When driving with Kevin, we would see the cars on the main street doing what locals called "The Waltzing Matilda," slipping and sliding all over the road. Some people got a great kick out of it. Not me, though, especially when I was in the driver's seat! There was one night in particular when I found myself not just waltzing—way worse, in fact. But for the grace of God, the children and I could have been very badly hurt. Thank God for seat belts and Angels!

The incident in question happened one bleak and deathly cold night. Kevin was flying in from Edmonton, and I wanted to surprise him with the children and myself at the airport to greet him. He would have had a fit if he thought I had driven in that black ice, and warned me against it. But I knew how lonely it felt arriving at an airport with nobody to greet you, and was sure I could do it, even though I was really nervous, and had never attempted that journey to the airport before.

After spending a good few minutes bundling up the children and myself, we left ourselves plenty of time to travel. It was a very dark night, and visibility was next to impossible. Fortunately, there were hardly any cars travelling on the road. It seemed like it was just the children, myself, and the great Milky Way above us.

I turned on some happy music to keep the girls amused, and then focused entirely on the driving. I needed to. I will admit I was frightened, especially when all I could feel was pure ice beneath me. It really was like driving on an ice rink. Was I crazy for attempting this? Yes, I was.

After a while, there was a clearing on the road and I was able to make some speed. Not such a wise idea on my part, because as soon as I hit the accelerator, the jeep spun completely out of control. This wasn't a waltz—more like a quick step! It all happened so fast. I remember my hands left the steering wheel, and I lost complete control. I was sure the vehicle was going to turn upside down, and that would be the end of us. It was a petrifying situation. Yet the car kept moving, even after all the skidding. Somebody else was steering that car for me—and it was you-know-who!—Angelica, my great celestial pal.

We ended up on the opposite side of the road, on an incline of some kind. It was covered in snow, so I don't know what planet we had landed on, but it was high, and I had to drive off it. Fortunately, there was no oncoming traffic. Can you imagine if there was? It was a miracle that none of us was hurt, and the car didn't get as much as a scratch—what are the odds?

I turned the car off completely, took a very deep breath, said a prayer of thanks to God and my Angel protectors, and asked them to please stay with me in the car until we got to the airport. I was closer to it now than home, so I may as well keep going. I don't think the children even knew what was happening. They were so young at the time. I think they were asleep in the back of the car, as there wasn't a sound out of them.

When I met Kevin at the airport, and he smiled and asked, "How's it going, darling?" I smiled back and said, "Perfect, darling—couldn't be better!" I'd wait and tell him once we got home safely!! We got there, and thank God I'm alive to tell the tale!

The Guinness Ghost

In the summer of 1986, I worked on a temporary basis for the renowned and greatly respected Guinness Corporation. It was a job "for life," or, as some folk dubbed it, the "fur-lined mouse trap." Mouse trap or not, it was a great place to work, and the company looked after their staff very well indeed. Benefits included a terrific salary, free medical care, free daily lunch, two free bottles of beer per day to bring home (not to drink on the premises!), education benefits, Christmas parties…and the list goes on. Male employees had no trouble finding a wife either ("Oh, so you work in Guinness?…Ahh!"). They were off to the races! Another wonderful fringe benefit.

In the early days, before female emancipation, lady employees of the brewery had to leave their employment as soon as they got married. Not fair, I agree, but that's the way it was. It was a plus for the male, and a minus for the female, to work for Guinness. Many women did not marry for that reason I am sure, as it was such a good job to have to give up, and money was tight. Sadly, they became known as "The Brewery Nuns."

"How did nuns get their name?" a male employee asked me one day. Not knowing, he told me—"They get 'None' Monday,

Tuesday, Wednesday, Thursday, Friday, Saturday or Sunday!"
The guys there had a great sense of humour—you'd need it!

By the time 1986 had arrived, things were swinging at the
brewery, and temps were allowed in through the golden gates
to paradise. It has to be admitted, just as a female was a lesser
citizen, so too were the "Temps." Temp or not though, the
money was great, and the lunch delicious. In addition, I became
very popular rambling home each night with two free bottles
of beer in my bag.

Fortunately, they liked me at the brewery, and I was a good
worker even if I say so myself. The powers that be wanted to
make me permanent, but there was just one teeny tiny hitch—I
had to prove my worth, and test my mettle. In other words, I had
to do a bit of suffering first…

On July 13, 1986, four days after my third wedding
anniversary, the company despatched me down to work at the
Guinness depot in Waterford. The office there was in dire need
of a "Girl Friday," as the previous lady had left in a mad hurry. It
was a tough station, but I knew I was up to the challenge—I had
to be! I was the only female in an office surrounded by men, but
they were all adorable, and made my time so pleasant. It wasn't
easy being away from Kevin, and the comforts of home, but I
got through it. Besides, a permanent job with Guinness was the
carrot before my donkey. And it was a juicy carrot at that.

Talk about getting thrown in at the deep end though!
Nobody ever asked me if I could drive. I guess they just assumed
I could. Besides, I did take driving lessons once a very long time
ago—that counts, doesn't it?! So when I was asked one day to

drive a faulty mechanic's car back up to Dublin to be fixed at the depot, my heart did a back flip. What could I do? Say no? I was in Waterford to prove my mettle, I thought, so I might as well feel the fear and do it anyhow. And as you know by now, I'm always game ball for a challenge!

The faulty car stalled at the top of a very steep hill in Waterford—just my luck! Why does this always happen when you're the first one in line? I forgot to tell you—not alone did I not have my full driving licence, but I couldn't really drive either. An enormous line of irate drivers had piled up behind me. I was sweating like a bull. Fortunately, Angelica came to my rescue. The man behind me was most helpful, and got the car going. Now it was up to me to *keep* it going. I think this was the first time I experienced an Angel driving the car for me. All I had to do was hold the steering wheel!

But if you think that was scary, wait 'til you hear about the Guinness Ghost! Had I known beforehand that the Guinness office in Waterford was haunted, I would never in a million years have taken up the challenge—or would I?

This is how I first met Mr. Ghost…

It was a balmy summer's evening in the brewery. I was busy in my office at the very top of the building—45 steps up in fact—without an elevator. It had been a very busy day, and I still had lots of work to complete. It was around 9 pm at the time. I had all the technical reps' large blue worksheets spread out neatly on the ground, and was checking them for errors. Lots of work to do if I was to get home before midnight! The old Waterford

Brewery is several hundred years old (which is why they had no elevator), and it was spooky into the bargain.

Suddenly, in the midst of my work, I could hear heavy footsteps walking up the stairs. What?! It was nearly 10:00 at night—who could be coming up at this hour of the night? The customers knew the office was closed at 6, and the employees in the offices below were always gone by 7. This was odd— very odd.

As the footsteps drew closer, they had a strange, hollow tone to them. The hair on the back of my neck literally stood up. I knew this was no ordinary person coming up those stairs—it could only be a ghost! There was nothing for a few flights up except my office and the small kitchenette on the landing, just outside my office door.

Picture the scene: I was standing in front of the door waiting for the ghost to come nearer, trembling like a leaf. As soon as the footsteps stopped outside the door, my heart was exploding inside of me. I had never felt such fear, and since the only other way down was via the window, there was nothing for it but to meet him face-to-face. Bravely, I opened up the door, and sure enough, there was nothing there. What greeted me was an icy cold breeze as if I had just opened a freezer. It encircled my head, like a genie being released from its bottle.

With the help of divine intervention, I spoke out loudly, and very clearly, to the entity: "Excuse me, but can you please go away. You are frightening me, and I have my work to do!" As soon as I said this, the ghostly genie whooshed back into his bottle, and disappeared, leaving me with an enormous feeling of peace and calm. I sensed the ghost did not want to upset me, and was most accommodating in that regard. I never had trouble again after that.

Needless to say, I gave the ghost enough time to go, grabbed my handbag, and literally flew down the 45 darkened stairs. Since it was such an old building, the lights kept flickering off, which was furiously frightening.

Upon enquiring, I was to learn later that yes, there was a ghost in the building, but that he was a "friendly ghost." I would agree with that.

You are Never Alone

Have you ever felt the heart-twisting ache of loneliness? If so, you are not alone. The number of people who report feeling lonely and isolated today has increased greatly over the years, despite the fact we live in a computer-controlled social media world—or maybe it's because of this. Facebook has replaced the telephone as a means of communication. And alas, the internet has gobbled up the world of greeting cards and snail mail. It's all about instant gratification now. But the question has to be asked: *is* it gratifying? Does social media *really* feed our soul?

You can feel alone in a crowded room, or in the privacy of your own bedroom. There is no explanation really—only solutions, we hope. Suicide is on the up and up, and so are obesity, drug addiction, alcoholism. They are all side effects of that highly contagious disease called loneliness, which spreads throughout the world, irrespective of borders and boundaries.

Facebook makes some people feel like losers, especially when they see their friends are all enjoying a rip roaring social life, which, as we all know, is hammed up for the audience. We need to look elsewhere for peace within.

As an emigrant living far from home for the past two decades, I can say with my hand on my heart that I'm an expert on Loneliness. I know the depths of despair to which the soul can sink. It can be brutal, for want of a better word.

I can recall feeling terribly lonely and isolated when I first arrived in Fort McMurray, some twenty years ago. I would do silly things, like when my shampoo bottle from Ireland's Dunnes Stores was empty, I would fill it up with the new shampoo I had bought. It made me feel at home to see the Dunnes Stores' price tag on the bottle! I was so far away from home, and the people around me were so different in temperament. I felt very much "an outsider."

I remember how happy I was to discover Mars Bars and Kit Kats in the shops, and all the familiar food from home. That was a bonus! I went to a Dana concert in Calgary some years later, and Dana spoke of her own similar experiences missing home, family, and the familiar comforts. She had been living in America for years. As she spoke of her experiences as an emigrant, in between songs, I could feel the tears rolling down my cheeks. When she sang "When Irish Eyes are Smiling," I was glad the room was dark and nobody could see me, because my eyes were far from smiling!

Over the years, I've had many a conversation with God as to why he wanted me to live in Canada, as opposed to Ireland, which would have been my first choice. My wise husband Kevin said the Universe teaches us the lessons we have to learn in this lifetime, and God is the Universe. I thought about it a lot, and came to the realization that if I had stayed in Ireland, my faith may not be as strong as it is today. It is only through suffering that you grow as a person, and hopefully in wisdom, too. The words of Jesus, "Suffer little children to come unto me," truly resonate with me.

One September morning, I can recall an incident when this message came to me loud, and very clear indeed...

The beginning of September was always my least favourite time of the year. The children would be returning to school, happy from their holidays in Ireland, and I would return to an empty house...missing them while they were at school, missing family. Feeling lonely.

Fortunately, we lived near the school, so the girls could come home at lunchtime, and I would walk them back to school. One day, I was *really* down in the dumps. The harsh Calgary winter was on its way, and I asked myself, "Is this all there is?" I just couldn't snap out of my gloomy mood. It happens!

Suddenly, as I walked along the street, my eyes caught the sight of a bright, glittery object on the grass. Curious, I reached down and picked it up. It was a large silver pendant, with the most strikingly beautiful picture of Jesus engraved onto it. There was a ray of sunshine surrounding his head. It was a striking piece, and the minute I held it in my hand, the gloomy mood completely disappeared—like magic! It was meant to be. Finding the medal at that moment in time was fortuitous and highly symbolic. The message transmitted to me that day was:

With Jesus by your side, you are never alone!

A Near Fiasco in France!

Over the years, I have plonked myself into some hair-raising situations, especially during my hitchhiking days. In retrospect, I was foolhardy—or simply insane! My adventurous streak dominated my brain, leaving little room for common sense. Thank God for Angels!

Of all the "close calls," there is one particular moment which I shall never forget. It shall remain in my memory simply because I felt the Angels fought a big battle on my behalf that night.

After our year in Paris had come to an end, my sister and I decided to invest in a little two-man tent and travel around a bit before heading to work on a Kibbutz in Israel. I can remember the excitement we felt on choosing our little brown tent. It was so cozy and light to carry. It did the job very well indeed. Since we were already in the country, we started off our adventures in France.

Our first port of call was in the picturesque town of Vannes, in Normandy. It was such a quaint and beautiful city. If the truth be known, I would have preferred to have been able to afford a hotel! It was raining non-stop, and we were huddled together, freezing in our little brown tent, eating chocolate biscuits and drinking cold water. Nowhere to plug in a kettle for tea. We were off to a rather chilly start.

We continued on our adventures until we arrived in the South of France. The weather by now was much warmer—in fact it was almost too hot! Somewhere along the way, we got chatting with a very friendly man we met in a café. We asked him about campsites, and for directions. He was indeed very helpful, and offered us the use of a big field at the back of his property. Since it was getting dark, he gave us the loan of his torch, which was a big, industrial type of lamp. I remember it was a heavy one, and I am sure an expensive one at that.

Because it was such a warm balmy evening, and late, we ended up not pitching our tent at all. Instead, we just spread out the little foam supports for our sleeping bags, and decided to sleep out beneath the lovely twinkly stars—how romantic was that?

So as not to get cold during the night, I was fully dressed inside the sleeping bag, with a warm hoodie on me. I put the hood around my head and made myself all snug and cozy, and then tried to sleep. My sister was out like a light, as she was very tired. Unfortunately, try as I might, I just could not sleep. Maybe I sensed impending danger!

Some time later, and still awake, I could hear the sound of heavy footsteps coming towards us. It definitely was a man, and a big one at that. As he got closer, a little voice inside me told me to put my head completely into the sleeping bag, which I did.

The man walked right up to where I was lying. I felt such a dreadful, strong sense of evil coming from him, despite the fact I could not even see him! He began to walk all around me, trying to see what gender I was—that is the sense I got. As I lay in the sleeping bag, with my head completely covered by the hoodie, it would have been difficult for him to see if I was male or female. I was petrified in case he saw me move. I tried to pretend I was asleep, and was afraid to breathe or make a sound. He kept eerily walking around my sleeping bag for what felt like a very long time.

I thought my heart would stop!

As he slowly walked around me, I prayed like I've never prayed before, that this strange, evil presence encircling me would please go away, and leave me alone. He hesitated for a moment, as if he was contemplating something, walked away, then came back again. I felt the Angels were putting up a good fight for my soul. A lot of negotiating was going on! Would he? Would he not? My body was rigid with fear as I tried to keep deadly quiet.

Unexpectedly, the stranger bent down beside my sleeping bag as if reaching for something—me? I thought my heart would give me away. I don't know how I kept it together. Miraculously, he stood up and walked away. I waited until I felt he was completely gone, before breathing a *huge* sigh of relief.

If he knew I was awake, and was a female, what would have happened? Exhausted, I simply nodded off after he left. There was no way I was moving out of that sleeping bag! The next morning I discovered that the mysterious intruder had stolen the torch lent to us by the owner of the field. The man was really annoyed. I don't think he believed me when I told him it had been stolen. Could *he* have been the mysterious "stalker"? I don't know—and never will. I am just so very grateful to be here to tell the tale!

Life on an Israeli Kibbutz

After our travels in Europe, we decided to go to Israel to work on a kibbutz. It was an adventure high on our bucket list of things to do. Because our French was pretty good at the time, we decided to head for a French-speaking kibbutz, called Baram, located on the Lebanese border. It was September 1978, and the weather was still very hot. We would start our work day picking fruit in the orchards at 5 am and finish by noon. Breakfast was huge, and consisted of a large selection of different foods, including fish. I thought it odd to start the day with fish, but soon got with the program.

The sight of war tanks and bomb shelters scattered around the kibbutz was a constant reminder that I was in a war zone, just in case I ever forgot! Despite this, I never really felt a sense of danger during my time on this kibbutz. As volunteers, we were treated well, and appreciated for our efforts to help in Israel. I was in awe of the incredible work ethic of the Israeli people. They had "before" and "after" pictures of the kibbutz, displayed in large, framed pictures on the canteen walls, and it was clear that a lot of sweat equity had gone into making the kibbutz the thriving place it was. As a French-speaking kibbutz, the settlers all originated from French-speaking countries, united by their Jewish heritage. There were many Swiss people living on the kibbutz, and it is true to say they ran it like clockwork!

Because it was located on the Lebanese border, there were certain dangers and limitations that I was not entirely aware of. For one, it was not advisable to walk alone at night in certain areas, for fear of being shot at!

One night, I was going to take a little stroll, but felt a strong warning from heaven not to. Just as well! A Dutch volunteer narrowly escaped being shot at. The poor unfortunate fellow was deaf, went for a jog, and did not hear the people shouting at him.

My abiding memory of Israel was how beautiful the country was, and I loved the city of Jerusalem. After Paris, it is my second favourite city in the world. I loved the rich culture and diversity of the people, and the magnificent golden Dome of the Rock was breathtaking. There was also something profoundly moving about visiting the city of Bethlehem, walking the same streets that Jesus had walked, and seeing the spot where he was born in the stable.

To see with my very eyes all the places I had heard about in the Bible, and to bathe in the same waters where Jesus had performed the miracle of the loaves and fishes was a truly unique experience. I enjoyed a mud bath in the Dead Sea, and tasted my first falafel wrap ever in Jerusalem. The falafel wraps in Israel are the best! Nobody else can make them like they do—they have the magic recipe.

When I visited Israel in 1978, the country was still raw from the wounds inflicted during the 1967 war between Israel and Palestine. There was still a lot of tension and hostility in the air between the Palestinians and Israelis. As a woman, I noticed a huge difference between the way an Israeli man treated me compared to a Palestinian man's treatment. Israeli men had a lot of respect for women, and I loved that about them. Unfortunately, and purely from a female perspective, I did not feel safe on my own around the Palestinian men. When walking down the street, they would cackle and make jeering sounds as I walked by. They clearly thought that because I was a foreign woman walking on my own I was nothing more than a "low-life."

One day, when I was walking on my own down a side street in Bethlehem, a group of Palestinian men passed me by, and honest to goodness, I had to run for cover! I remember thinking to myself I wouldn't like to meet them down a dark alley way late at night! I felt very frightened and intimidated by their aggressive behaviour towards me.

Unfortunately, I was to have a similar experience some weeks later, and but for my Angels being there to protect me, I may not have had such a lucky escape!

I was working on a Brazilian kibbutz in the south of the country when the incident in question happened. This kibbutz was as different from the previous one as night is from day, in that it was very laid-back, carelessly managed, and not as clean either. Also, to my great disappointment, I discovered that a lot of the hunky foreign volunteers were gay! It was nicely located, however, and the countryside around was very pretty.

One day, I got the loan of a bicycle from the volunteers' office, and decided to go for a cycle on my own. I can remember cycling for hours down back-country lanes, and loving the intoxicating feeling of freedom, with the sun in my face and a gentle breeze caressing my hair as I cycled along the country roads.

I can remember singing aloud one of my favourite Beatles' songs: "I was alone, I took a ride, I didn't know what I would find there…" I was having so much fun, with not a fear or care in the world! But it wasn't to last for long…

Suddenly, a truck filled with the same kind of jeering men I had encountered in Bethlehem drove along by me. When they saw me, they stopped the truck and began to jeer and mock me. The look on their faces said it all! Two of the men got out of the truck, and made their way towards me. To say I was frightened was an understatement! There is no knowing what their intentions were. I was alone and vulnerable on a country road.

Suddenly, my Angels kicked into action. It's such a wonderful feeling to know there is somebody looking out for you, even if you cannot see them. The driver of the truck began to shout at the men in a foreign language I did not understand. Clearly, he did not like their behaviour, and felt they were out-of-line. He must have instructed them to get back into the truck, because that is exactly what they did. Was I lucky or what? The driver smiled at me (he was a good guy), and off they drove, leaving me unharmed.

I breathed a huge sigh of relief as their truck drove away. I got back on my bike, and pedalled all the way back to the kibbutz. Needless to say, I never went out for a bike ride on my own again!

Blinded by the BMW!

It's true to say that you can never judge a book by its fancy cover! That is the lesson my sister and I learned the day we accepted a ride from a German man driving a swish, shiny BMW. Naturally, when this fancy car stopped to offer us a ride as we were hitching from Italy to Austria, we were happy to accept. It was a lovely sunny day, and promised to be a pleasant journey.

We had a long day ahead of us, as our driver was going to bring us all the way from Italy to Austria—how lucky was that! Like most German businessmen, he spoke perfect English, so the conversation flowed easily, and for the most part, pleasantly. We stopped for a few breaks along the way, and there was absolutely no indication that he was anything but a pure gentleman. He liked the fact we were Irish, and sisters. That appealed to him. We were good conversationalists, and helped speed up the journey for him as well. So really, when all was said and done, it was a win-win situation for everybody involved—or so we innocently thought!

As the day progressed, the weather changed dramatically. While it had been sunny and warm in Italy, it was pouring rain as we approached Innsbruck, Austria. We had nothing but sundresses on us, and it was getting cold.

Just as the weather changed, so too did the manner of our driver. The tone of his voice changed from light and breezy to dark and serious. He explained that he was going to be stopping in a hotel for the night, as it was getting late, and invited us to stay with him. What? I wondered to myself…was he suggesting? Did I hear correctly? Apparently yes.

He wanted all three of us to stay in the same hotel room, and he would "pay for everything." "You mean the two of us to stay in the same room, or the same bed?" I had to clarify. "The same bed," he replied. "It will be pleasant, and you can leave in the morning, with everything paid for, including breakfast," he continued in his matter-of-fact voice. Like as if he did this on a regular basis. Did he know we were sisters? Catholic? Did he not see the rosary beads we wore close to our chest, as a protectant?

As the older sister, my job was to protect us. I was having none of this ménage-a-trois thing—absolutely not! I felt cheap, and was disappointed that our pleasant journey had to come to such a peculiar end.

"I'm sorry, but we are Irish Catholic girls, and don't do that sort of thing!" I said to him, thinking he would understand, and just laugh it off. No such luck! Suddenly, his face darkened with anger once he realized I was serious, and not going to comply with his wishes. He stopped the car, and then roared at us, "Get out of ze car! Now!"

I could see from the look in his eyes that he meant it! He was livid with rage, and showed zero compassion for us poor sisters, stranded in the middle of nowhere, in the dark of night, the rain pouring down upon us, and wearing light, sleeveless summer dresses. We had to drag our bags from the back of his car. Mr. Nasty was not in the mood for social pleasantries, or for helping us out. No, he wanted us to suffer. As soon as we had all our belongings, off he drove at a great speed. I would not have liked to have been on my own in his car when he made his indecent proposal.

Alone now, and in the middle of nowhere, I could once again feel the hands of Angels helping us out. When I told you I kept them busy, I meant it! We reached for our little brown tent, and managed to clumsily put it together. Though not perfectly assembled, at least it afforded us a roof over our heads until morning came, and we could see where we were. We had no food or water with us, so it was a long, dark night! Still, the alternative accommodation with Mr. Nasty was far less appealing.

When morning came, we could see that we were in fact not too far from the city of Innsbruck in Austria. We managed to make our way to a petrol station, and soon everything was all rosy in the garden again.

The moral of the story: Never judge a book by its shiny, swish cover. Appearances can be deceptive.

Holy Communion Day, May 1964

Paris, Here I Come! Summer 1977

My First Paris Metro Ticket, 1977

A Busy Day at My Multinational Language College, Paris 1977

Hanging Out with Little Sis and Friends, Paris 1977/78

A Day in the Life of a Hitchhiker, Germany 1978

Sister Sonya and Me, Rome 1978

Two Sisters and Two Camels, Morocco 1978

Disaster at the Dead Sea, Israel 1978.

The Mystery of the Medals

I cannot understand why all my life I have been finding medals, and in the strangest of places, too! I wanted to write a chapter on it, because I find it odd, and perhaps there is a good reason for it.

It all began when I found my First Holy Communion medal at the age of seven—that was a happy find! The next significant medal was a surprise present from my husband Kevin, when we first began dating. I had never mentioned a single word to him; never even dropped as much as a hint! Besides, giving your girlfriend a medal wasn't a typical gift to give a girl. In my heart of hearts, I longed to have a really nice gold Miraculous Medal, so you can imagine my surprise when one day, totally unexpected, he presented me with the most beautiful gold Miraculous Medal. Thirty years later, I'm still wearing it. He was surely inspired!

Then there was that day in Calgary, when I was feeling really down in the dumps. I was walking along the street when I found a beautiful medal of the Sacred Heart of Jesus, with a halo of sunshine around his head. It was just there sitting in the grass, waiting for me! Talking about grass, another day I was taking a photo at my sister's wedding. My high heel got stuck in the grass and actually came off my foot—how embarrassing! I had to wrench it out of the earth, and what should I find stuck into the mud? Yes, a lovely medal of Our Lady! That's what I meant when I said I find them in the oddest of places.

When we went back to Ireland several years ago, it was with the intention of staying. We went to look at a house in Galway which was for sale. It seemed perfect, but the engineer who checked the property had major concerns, so we never went ahead. As we walked around the garden in this charming country house, I found a most beautiful medal stuck in the grass. I took it as a sign that Our Lady was in control. She was watching over this most difficult of decisions for us. We ended up returning to Canada after our year in Galway, and just finding that little medal was all the assurance I needed that we were being guided, and I knew in my heart that we had made the right decision. God has a plan for us, and he has his ways for letting me know.

I have always had a very deep devotion to Our Lady, so when a work colleague told me many years ago that her mother—who also had a very strong devotion to our Lady—was always finding medals, a light bulb went off in my head. Was it co-incidence or what?

The most recent medal I found was a beautiful gold one, and it had a lovely image of the Sacred Heart of Jesus on it. Guess where I found this one? I found it on the ferry one day, on my way from Victoria to Vancouver. Who would have thought? People were walking over it as it lay on the ground where the cars are parked in the oily bowels of the ferry. I saw it and initially thought that it was my own Miraculous Medal which had fallen off me.

So be on the lookout—you just never know where you may find one. If you do find a special medal, ask yourself is it co-incidence? Or maybe it is God trying to speak to you?

DIY *Angel Power*

I'm always on the lookout for messages from my Angels, be it in the form of a bumper sticker on a car, a message on a billboard, or a random fortune cookie message I find on the street. However, when I want to touch or feel my Angels, I reach for one of my animals. They are heaven sent and that is for sure.

Animals give you their undivided love and devotion 24/7. If you are having a difficult day, you can talk to your pet, and you can be sure they are hearing what you say. They slow you down, and insist that you take time to smell the roses. They are God's little messengers of love. I believe that every dog or cat that comes into your life was meant to. If you want to feel closer to God and to have your own living, breathing Angel, invest in an animal – better still, maybe consider adopting one from a shelter. It could be a win win situation for all concerned.

I understand that many folk renting may not be permitted to have a pet, which is a pity. In that case, you can still create your own "Angel Space."

Find yourself a little unoccupied space, and a small table. Ideally near a window, or even your dressing table. I have a space in the basement which I use for the purpose of prayer and contemplation. The small room was once occupied by the cook when our house was first built in 1916. Now it houses all my holy stuff, statues, candles, music, and Angels – lots of Angels.

When I didn't have the luxury of a room to myself, I would use a small table and simply put my statues and candles on that. The simple act of lighting a candle and watching the flame flicker transports you to a place of peace and calm. Listening to soft angelic music will help release the tensions of the day, and settle you down for a quiet time of prayer and contemplation. Add some sweet incense and now you have a fragrant garden. Tessa, my cat loves to sit on my lap and play with my rosary beads. I tell her she is the holiest cat I know.

Give me these simple pleasures and I'm in heaven. Simplicity is the operative word. You can create your own heavenly space with little difficulty, and lots of enjoyment.

Saved by an Angel!

When I stop and think about life, I wonder at all the many narrow escapes I have had, and I thank God for sending me his Angels, and for their loving protection.

There is one incident that comes to mind where but for the grace of God and divine intervention I would most definitely not be alive today. Let me tell you about it, and you will see exactly what I mean.

The incident in question happened over the May long weekend some years ago. My daughter Victoria was making her Confirmation, and her godmother, my sister Sonya, had come over for the occasion. On the day before my sister's departure, I awoke with a strong feeling that we should get away for the day.

There was an urgency about the feeling I was having—it was more like an instruction from heaven. I've had these "angelic orders" before, so I knew better than to ignore it. When a thought or feeling comes to your head, you know there must be a reason for it. Many survivors of plane crashes and other disasters will tell you of suddenly changing their plans at the last moment, thus avoiding tragedy.

Without thinking, I just said to everybody, "Let's go to Vancouver for the day." It was all very random, and certainly not planned. So, off we all headed for Vancouver, and a fun day was had by all.

We returned to a very strong wind storm in Victoria. Trees had shed large branches all over the roads. Strong gale force winds shook our car from side to side, making it a tense, white knuckle drive all the way home. Little did we expect what awaited us…

When we arrived at our home, police cars were flashing their lights outside, sirens were going, and people were standing on the street looking in through the hedges. The rain was pounding down. My first thought was that we must have been robbed. We drove up to the policemen and explained that we lived in the house and asked that the heck was going on. "You'd better be very careful," he said, explaining that a huge oak tree had fallen on our house and had crashed into the living room. All the wires were exposed and we were in danger of being electrocuted because of the rain.

Our house was off the road and on a private lot so we couldn't see the immediate damage, but when we went in the sight that awaited us was one I will not forget in a hurry. The tree that fell was a huge 150-year-old oak tree, and if we were in the house when it happened at 9 pm there is no way anybody in the room would have survived. The roof had caved in, and the tree was resting on the coffee table. The insurance man said he never in his life had seen such a tree disaster!

Apparently the noise from the tree falling on the house was so loud that even an elderly, deaf neighbour had heard it and came out to investigate!

The moral of the story is, of course, always listen to your Angels!

But the story does not end here. After the initial shock had subsided, we all consoled ourselves that nobody had been hurt, our precious dogs were safe and well, and insurance would cover the enormous costs of rebuilding the living room. I relaxed somewhat, even though I was frustrated because we had just finished decorating that room after a year of renovations from Hell! Now we had to face all that again…what a thrilling thought!

God gives you the strength when you need it most, though, and I'm a firm believer that there is always a reason for things happening…

When the chimney mason came to rebuild our collapsed chimney, he was horrified to discover that the chimney was actually very dangerous. He said it was a miracle that it had not gone on fire already. In fact, he said if the tree had not knocked down the chimney and front room, we may have had a serious fire on our hands. And if the Angels had not guided me to go to Vancouver that day…well now that would have been a very different story too!

Talk about a tree saving our house! God certainly works in the most mysterious of ways, but boy, does he work, and in the end it's all good.

Finding Mr. Right

Thankfully, I didn't have to kiss many frogs before I met my handsome prince! Our story is an unusual one, and I believe it was meant to be.

I was just ten years old when Kevin first walked into my life. At that moment in time, he wasn't Mr. Right, though, more like "Mr. Wrong!" He was new to our town—his family had just moved home from Canada to settle in my hometown in the west of Ireland. When we met at the age of ten, Kevin was trespassing with his brother Tom and a friend at the "private club" my sisters and I ran in a turf shed at the back of a pub! Since my maiden name was Hayes, we aptly called it the "Hazelnut Club!" (Later, my father-in-law would jokingly call Kevin and me "KP Nuts" after a popular brand of peanuts). The boys were teasing us because they had a packet of delicious pink wafer biscuits, and we weren't getting any!

By the age of 12, I thought Kevin was "nice" and two years later, at the age of 14, I remember telling my grandmother that I had met the man I wanted to marry—no kidding! (Despite the fact we had never even as much as spoken to each other.) I had a massive crush on him for two very awkward adolescent years.

He used to do the readings in church, and a great job he did. I wasn't listening—just observing!

At 14, I went to my very first disco. I was pathologically shy, so when Kevin came over and asked me to dance, my poor legs were frozen to the spot. I was too shy to look at him, and instead—horror of horrors—said, "No thanks, I'm not dancing." Watching him walk back over to where the boys sat, my heart sank. I was so mad with myself! There was the love-of-my-life asking me to dance, and I had stupidly blown it! You can imagine my surprise when he came over and asked me again—he wasn't taking no for an answer. How romantic is that! This time I was pushed up by some helpful girl sitting behind me—"Get up and dance! You just put one leg in front of the other!"

We just innocently danced. Back then in the ice age, "nice girls" didn't go home with boys after a dance! They had to defer gratification. So after the dance was over, we went our separate ways, and it was to be a long time before our paths crossed again. I always carried a torch for this fellow, though, and never dated another, apart from one brief work encounter.

It was just that nobody else could hold candlelight. Despite the fact that we had only ever danced at the hops and once shared a lemonade, it was enough to convince me that he was "the one," the only one for me!

Because I never dated, people were convinced I was going to be a nun. At one point my mother was quite concerned for me, because I wasn't making any efforts to go out and socialize. She wanted me to meet nice fellows who were good marriage material. What was the point? I thought. I had already met "the one" and nobody else could match him for perfection!

In 1981, something very strange happened. I was 24 at the time, and surprise, surprise—still single. My sister Yvonne got married in January of 1981, and I was thrilled when she asked me to be her bridesmaid. We have an old superstition in Ireland that if you put a piece of wedding cake under your pillow, you will dream of the man you will marry. I did exactly that—I put a piece of her cake under my pillow, and had the most vivid dream that I was going to marry Kevin, and that we would spend many years travelling, away from our own country. Our lives together appeared before my eyes in a kaleidoscope of images. This was no ordinary dream—it was a prophecy, of that I was sure! It was not like an ordinary dream.

Two months after the dream, I went home to celebrate the long St. Patrick's weekend with my family in the West. My mother nagged me to within an inch of my life—"Get out there and mingle, or you'll end up an auld maid!" In desperation, I grabbed my 80-year-old grandfather, and the two of us headed out to the local hotel.

My hair was greasy and I had made no effort to dolly myself up, but believe it or not—I had the *best* night of my life! I had two different fellows wanting to buy me a drink! Kevin was there…but he had another Patricia in tow—not me this time! He came straight over to talk to me, and I could tell the little flame was still flickering. But because he was with somebody else, I wouldn't go near him! And that was the end of that. If it was meant to be, it would happen. My mother has a wonderful saying, which I regularly quote to my children, "What's meant for you will not go by you."

Meeting Kevin was not the most memorable event which happened to me that fateful evening in 1981, however. No, it was meeting his sister Susan, who had been in my class at school. Susan was a beautiful girl, and had just qualified as a lawyer. She came over to me, very friendly, to chat about our lives, and to introduce me to her then fiancé Tom, also a lawyer. As soon as I shook hands with her, an icy feeling came over my whole body. It was so sudden, and totally unexpected. I got a desperately lonely feeling when I held Susan's hand. In short, I saw no future for her—no children. In fact, I thought that maybe she and Tom were going to split up. I saw no future for them together. As I said, it was a most peculiar sensation, and one I will never forget.

A few short months later, on the 17th of July, Susan tragically died from a brain tumour. After her death, I could not get her out of my mind. Every night I would have recurring dreams about her. In the dreams, she was my sister—we shared clothes, and were very close.

Out of the blue one day, Kevin got in touch with me. He asked if he could write to me. He was no longer dating and we lived in different towns. The way events panned out, I felt like invisible hands from heaven were drawing us closer together. Our courtship was short—we got engaged in November 1982, and were married the following July. As soon as we got engaged, the dreams about Susan completely went away. We celebrated our 30th wedding anniversary this past July.

There are so many things about this life of ours which I will never ever fully understand. I just know one thing—*some things are meant to be*! I always keep an open mind. When a German psychic in Calgary once told me that my husband and I had been together in two past lives, and that it was our destiny to return to Canada, I began to wonder... He also mentioned that we had been Native Indians living in Manitoba. Could this explain the fascination both of us have always had with the Native Indian culture? When we first moved to Canada, we went all out and bought a life-sized wooden statue of an Indian, dream catchers, Indian artwork, listened to Buffy Sainte-Marie's music non-stop—you name it, we did it! And that was years before hearing we were supposed to have been Indians in a past life together! Cooincidence or what?

A Parent's Worst Nightmare

I love my three daughters with every fibre of my being. Not a day goes by that I don't thank God for the love and joy they have brought into our lives. Because they grew up without extended family in Canada, the bond between us is very tight. As they say around these parts, "We have each other's backs."

So you can imagine the way I felt the day my little Shirley Temple of a daughter, Victoria, disappeared. She was only three at the time, and a beautiful little doll, with a mop of blonde curly locks, and big blue eyes that would melt a stone. As a parent, it was naturally my worst nightmare!

On the day in question, we were shopping in one of the largest shopping malls in Canada, the West Edmonton Mall. The post-Christmas crowds in search of bargains were so dense we could barely move without being jostled from side to side. We were all walking beside each other at the time, or so I thought. Suddenly, my instinct (more like my Angel!) told me to turn around, and as I did, I noticed that our little Victoria was no longer with us. She was nowhere to be seen. I could feel myself swoon and am surprised I did not pass out with the shock of it. Where could she have gone? We knew nobody, and nobody knew us. Where would we even begin to look? It was absolutely, and without doubt, the worst day of my life.

As my body began to shudder, and my heart went out of control, I felt an invisible arm wrap itself around me in comfort. An Angel voice in my head said, "Do not panic—everything will be all right." I was frantic as I looked around at all the hundreds and thousands of strangers milling about. Whatever about me, what must Victoria be feeling? The poor child must be petrified. I just wanted to find her, and put my arms around her in comfort.

Thanks to my Angel support, I stayed surprisingly calm, as I knew they had her in their arms somewhere—but where? Now *that* was the big question. I had to enlist the help of St. Anthony on this particular assignment. I usually pray to him to help me find a lost object, but never a lost child!

"Let's backtrack," I told Kevin in the calmest voice I could muster. His face was deathly pale. He too was petrified with fear. So, pushing one-year-old Claudia in her pushchair, with Kevin carefully holding our eldest daughter Ali's hand, we battled our way through the throngs of shoppers. Please God, St. Anthony, my Angels—please help us find Victoria safely, I pleaded. Put us out of our misery! Believe me, five minutes in that situation is like five hours!!

We went back into every shop we had entered before losing our little darling. I listened intently to the calm directions from my Angels. I knew they would not let me down. They never have. They led me exactly where I needed to go to find Victoria.

Sounds strange I know, but it was as if an Angel walked beside me telling me where to go.

Suddenly, from the corner of my eye, I spotted her royal highness sitting on a chair in a shoe shop we had been into earlier. Even at that very young age, she loved shoes! She was surrounded by a host of admirers, with everybody fussing over her and being very nice, and a chocolate bar in her hand. She was smiling and happy.

Thank you God, Thank you God, Thank you God! That is all I could say over and over again, with tears of gratitude streaming down my face. If you are a mother or a father reading this, you know exactly the feeling in my heart when I saw my darling 3-year-old safe! Sadly, stories like this do not always end so happily. Never, ever take your eyes off your child. Having only two hands, and three children, I later bought a harness to use when travelling without Kevin. I never wanted to experience that feeling again!

The Angels were holding my hand that day, and clearly Victoria's too! Were it not for their soothing directions in my ears, and their warm invisible arms around my family, our story may not have ended too sweetly.

Part Two

Your Story: How to Connect with Your Angels

BELIEVE AND YOU SHALL RECEIVE

Have you ever wondered why we have two of everything? Two hands, two feet, two ears… Ok, I know we only have one head, but there are two eyes in it! My theory, based simply on my life experiences, is that one is for earth, and one for heaven. One for me, and one for my Angel. We are a pair, and the sooner you make friends with your very own celestial companion, the richer your life shall be. We really cannot do this life, with all its toil and turmoil, without some divine intervention. Two is far better company than one—it doubles the pleasure, and lessens the load.

In the following pages, I shall outline some suggestions on how best to connect with *your* Angel guides. Keep it simple, but keep it real.

I have a complete family of Angels that I pray to, including the more familiar, saintly ones (Matthew, Mark, Luke and John) and the Archangels (Michael, Gabriel, Raphael and Uriel). In addition, I pray to my own personal astrological Angel to help me realize my full potential as determined by my star sign, and to help steer me away from the shadow side. This can be a pretty empowering thing to do.

As you begin your journey of connection, I'd suggest you treat yourself to a really nice journal. To add to the experience, try and find a picture of an Angel that really appeals to you, and stick it on the cover. You could download one from your computer, or find one from an old Christmas card.

The next step may take a little longer. Focus on your Angel guide, and ask them for a name… I know it may seem strange, but trust me—it works! The first name that comes to you is the name of your Angel guide. You may need to *really* concentrate on this part. Asking them to reveal their name to you requires a quiet mind, free of all distractions. Remember that your Angel was right there beside your crib, from the moment you uttered your first cry. He or she has been sent by God, and specially chosen for you, and you alone.

Let's say the name that came to you, after deep contemplation, was Angelina. Congratulations! Now you have opened the dialogue with your very own personal Angel. Keep the conversation going. Instead of writing "Dear Diary" in your journal, start each entry with "Dear Angelina…"

When you've had an absolutely rotten day at work and your new boss is making your life a misery; when you feel you have nobody to turn to, or feel sad, lonely, overweight or underpaid, et cetera, et cetera, what you need is a forever friend, a leave-me-never-friend. This is where your Angel comes in.

As your journaling continues, please ponder on the following questions, and answer them with complete honesty. That's the lovely thing about your Angel guide—you can be your absolute and complete self, warts and all, and they are going to love you all the same.

The following questions will help you keep it real, and maybe get the old engine going:

- Are you happy for most of the time?
- Is your mind at peace?
- Do you believe in a higher power?
- Are your mind, body, and soul in harmony?
- Do you suffer from addictions? Alcohol? Drugs? Spending? Food? Gambling? Sex? Nicotine? Etc.
- Are you lonely?
- Is your job fulfilling?
- Have you found your true calling?
- Are you in a harmonious relationship with a significant other?
- If your fairy Godmother allowed you to have one wish fulfilled, what would it be?

But life is not that easy, is it? No fairy Godmothers-for-hire website that I know of. No Prince Charming to find our missing slipper. But fear not… There is a power *far greater* than any fairy Godmother or Prince Charming, and that is the power of our Angels.

For more than five decades, I have tried and tested their power. My true life experiences, from the age of seven onwards have left me in no doubt—absolutely no doubt whatsoever—that Angels really and truly do exist. And the great news is they are free for all!

CREATE A SACRED SPACE

Keeping a journal is a good way to start communicating with your Angel guides, but to really enhance your connection, you may want to consider creating a sacred space devoted to all things spiritual somewhere in your home.

You will need:

- *Sacred space to create a little home altar*
- *Small table and cloth*
- *Scented candles*
- *Angel statues that appeal to you*
- *Crystals*
- *Angel cards for reading, which you can buy at any good bookstore*
- *Angel statues—as many as you want. Try to find an Archangel Michael statue as he is all-powerful, and deserves a place on your altar!*
- *Soft, angelic music*
- *And whatever else takes your fancy!*

TAKE TIME TO MEDITATE

First thing in the morning, before you start your day, call upon your Angel protectors to guide, guard, and protect you and your loved ones that day. Shuffle your Angel cards, choose a card, and meditate on the message it delivers for the day.

I guarantee if you start your day with a little prayer to your Angels, they will stay by your side. Later, I will share some of my favourite Angel prayers with you.

PERFORM AN EVENING RITUAL

In the evening before going to bed, please try to turn off your computer at least an hour before your nightly ritual, to relax your mind. Make yourself a nice cup of relaxing herbal tea or hot chocolate. Remember, this is *you* time, and it will help ease you into a restful night's sleep. As you sip your bedtime brew, light a little scented candle on your Angel altar, and thank your Angels for their love and protection that day. I find lavender or vanilla-scented candles help get me in the mood for relaxation.

SHOW YOUR GRATITUDE

Angels like to be appreciated and thanked. They are beacons of light and love who love working with people who are grateful for the simple things in their lives, and who are generous in sharing what they have with others less fortunate. In short, they want you to be a good and kind person, too. They will give you a lot, but in return, you need to earn some good karma brownie points.

INDULGE IN SOME QUIET TIME

You will never hear your Angels whisper in your ears unless you make time in your day to be quiet—*really quiet*. Concentrate on the questions you may wish to ask them. Focus on one question at a time, and you will get your answer. It may come to you via your Angel cards, or it could be through a stranger way, perhaps via a fortune cookie message you may find in a random spot or a message on a car bumper sticker.

GAIN KARMA BROWNIE POINTS

Let's say you have a desire to find a soulmate, or that fabulous new job, new house, etc. It is not enough to simply ask your Angels for help. You need to go out, perform random acts of kindness, and *give give give*. The more you give to others, the better you will feel about yourself, and you will also be building a nice nest egg of karma. When the Angels get involved with your request for help, the response from heaven will be quicker if you have a good stash of karma brownie points! I truly believe that's how it works.

Magic happens when you give of yourself to others in a selfless way. I've experienced it for myself, so you're hearing it from the horse's mouth! Whenever I extend myself for others, the rewards frequently outnumber the effort expended. I find myself thinking less of myself, so yay! Less to worry about! It's a good feeling. God and Angels are very fair in that area. You give one, they give you two in return.

Even though there have been many times in my life when I have wanted to reach out and hug my Angels with every fibre of my being, I realized early on that the best way I could thank my beloved celestial friends was simply by baking up some delicious karma brownie points.

The joy you get when you give that beggar on the street a five dollar bill, a breakfast muffin and a wish for a happy day is especially delicious to your Angel. That's triple the karma brownie points! Helping out in a soup kitchen maybe once a week or even once a month, is a nourishing experience for the soul and heart warming for your Angel. Donating old clothing or unwanted gifts to the homeless shelter will bring another big smile to your Angel's face…and will earn you a decent amount of brownie points.

You probably get the idea by now—when you give, you get in return. The wheel of life swings with a smile, and life chugs along nicely. When you do goodly deeds, it is you who reaps even greater benefits than the recipient of your kindness.

FIND YOUR SOULMATE WITH THE ANGELS' HELP

When it comes to love, remember these words of wisdom:

> *"Follow love and it flees from thee, flee from love and it follows thee."*

If you don't start from a place of self-love, it is a waste of time looking for love externally. For one thing, you are putting a huge burden on another to make you happy! It is a really simple concept, highly effective, but unfortunately few realize it. Learn to like yourself. After all, it's true, you're going to be spending more time with yourself, than anybody else on earth– apart from your Angels!

A lack of self-connection, which leads to self-love, is part of the reason our world is awash with divorce, self-inflicted pain, suicide, etc. No, it is not selfish to love yourself – au contraire, it is a responsible thing to do. Loving yourself takes a lot of time. Unfortunately, for some, the journey is never-ending. It helps *enormously*, to have your Angel on board *the love train!*

It took me years to like myself. I took a bit of a pounding at school, and ended up feeling like an ugly duckling dunce, with two left legs, and ears bigger than my brain. Nasty stuff. One teacher in frustration used to call me *Paddy Last,* and I did everything in my power to live up to her expectations!

As a teenager, and young adult, I had such self loathing, I realized I was in no shape to go out looking for a soul-mate, besides, there was a lot of life to be lived. Once the school gates slammed behind me, and the sluice gates of life opened up before me, shimmering with wondrous potential, I began my journey to reclaim the power unkindly stripped from me at school.

Little did I know that as a pathologically shy 12-year-old, I had already met my future husband. How was I to know? We bumped into each other by chance when his parents stopped me in the street one day for directions. Because of his father's work, my prince charming arrived from Canada to live in our small town in the West of Ireland. His sister was in my class at school, and I thought he was the most handsome fellow in the world – and still do some forty years later!

By age 14, I was convinced he was "the one." At age 15 – he left again. His family moved from our small town, and my heart was shattered in a million pieces. We never spoke, apart from the odd dance at the local disco. He didn't know that I liked him, as I was too shy to let on. He left the town not knowing that I liked him, and that he liked me.

Fast forward ten years…

By now I was 25. Never really had a fellow. Never bothered to look for one. The torch had been kept aflame for '*the one*'.

I had done all my travelling, as you know from reading my adventure stories in part one of this book. I had earned my living in good sensible administrative office jobs, worked hard, and did well. No pain, no gain. The entire ten years was spent trying to build up a good relationship with myself. It took time, but thanks to prayer, and my fantastic Angels, it worked.

I woke up one day – miracle of miracles – I liked myself! Yay! I was ready to find myself a soul-mate. My figure was good, the skin was clear, my hair was long and glossy. I was well and truly ready. But no, I did not go actively seeking a mate. Instead, I prayed my guts out, did a novena to Our Lady of Good Counsel, who I absolutely love, because she has granted me numerous miracles, went to church when others were going to discos. And guess what? She sent "the one" right back into my path. The way it all happened left me in absolute no doubt that it smacked of divine intervention!

In summary – to find your soul-mate, you must obey the following rules:

Begin by learning to love yourself. Enjoy being in your own company.

Become comfortable in your own skin – warts and all.

Employ the help of Prayer and Angelic Power to find "the one".

Do not actively seek a mate, like you would a job. It could backfire!!

The day you realize you are happy, with or without a mate – love is on his/her merry way to join the party!! Take that as a clue.

Happy and contented people are easy to be around. They have a certain glow about them. They make you feel relaxed and comfortable. In short, they are a blessing in our lives. What's their secret? Cadbury's chocolate? Perhaps.

Prayer? Definitely!

Part Three

Angels & Astrology

There are lots and lots of Angels, and only enough hours in the day to pray to them all, so I like to keep it as simple as possible, and I focus on the Angels I find the most powerful, plus my Astrological Angel, which I will get to a little later. The following four prayers should be included in your daily Angel prayer ritual. You can recite them in the car to work, or any time you feel the need in your day.

ARCHANGEL MICHAEL – PROTECTOR AGAINST EVIL

I just love Archangel Michael. Too bad I never had a son. If I did, he would have been a Michael for sure! I recite the following prayer religiously each day. I wear his medal around my neck, on my keyring, and his name on my lips. Whenever I come across 'toxic' energy, either in the workplace, or externally, I whisper this well known prayer to myself. Here goes:

St. Michael the Archangel, defend me in my hour of need.

Be my safeguard against the wickedness and snares of the devil.

May God restrain him, we humbly pray, and do thou o prince of the heavenly host, by the power of God, cast into hell Satan, and all the evil powers who prowl about this world for the ruin of souls.

AMEN

ARCHANGEL URIEL – SURROUND ME WITH TRUE FRIENDS

Whenever I am having difficulties with friends, or find myself in a position wishing for more support, I always call upon Archangel Uriel before heading out to a party or place where I am meeting strangers.

Archangel Uriel, I call upon your tender mercy to guide good friends into my life. Protect me from false friends. Let those people who come into my life be kind, and genuine friends, who have only my best interests at heart. In turn, let me be an equally good and understanding friend to them.

For this I thank you.

As a writer, I call upon Archangel Gabriel on a regular basis. If I am having a writers' block, or am in need of some creative stimulation, I call upon Archangel Gabriel to fuel my imagination and help get the flow of creativity going again. He always comes through for me.

ARCHANGEL GABRIEL – ANGEL OF CREATIVITY

Archangel Gabriel, I call upon your tender mercy this day to help me to be creative in my words and deeds. Help my communication skills to be a blessing and inspiration to others.
For this I thank you.

Looking after my health is something I admit to being a bit careless about. I enjoy all the yummy food like cake, chocolate, ice cream and chips! I don't always exercise as much as I should. I am also careless about allowing stressful thoughts to enter into my private space – often without my permission and it sure drags me down. When this happens, or when I am starting a new health regime, I always call upon Archangel Raphael to help me to be disciplined with food and exercise and stress. He always helps!

ARCHANGEL RAPHAEL – ANGEL OF HEALING

> *Archangel Raphael, I call upon your tender mercy to help me to have a healthy mind in a healthy body. Help me to find peace within. Guide me in my choice of food. Help me to exercise more, and to respect my body.*
>
> **For this I thank you.**

If you say these brief prayers to the Archangels each morning, you'll be off to a great start!

ASTROLOGY, RELIGION, AND ANGELS

For centuries, Religion and Astrology have been the topics of much heated discussion, and they still are to this day. In both camps, there are "believers" and "non-believers." Personally, I'm a believer in all three: Astrology, Religion, and Angels.

My spiritual journey began at a young age. I was raised Roman Catholic, experienced my first Angel miracle at the tender age of seven, and discovered Astrology when I was 12. I have had a life-long devotion to Our Lady, the Holy Spirit, the Sacred Heart of Jesus, and countless Saints, Angels, and Archangels. They are my sanctuary and refuge in times of trial and tribulation…and by golly, I've put them to very good use in my life!

We have been travelling together for nearly five decades now, and I really cannot imagine what my life would have been like without their support.

So how did you first become interested in Astrology?

This is a question I get asked over and over again. I was 12 at the time of what I call my second "epiphany." The first was finding the Holy Communion medal and the second was opening up my first Astrology book. Both experiences had a profound effect on me.

When I first discovered Astrology, I was a pathologically shy and awkward 12-year-old—misery was my middle name! I felt a complete freak, especially since my other sisters were more outgoing and completely different from me. I wasn't the only one who noticed this; others commented as well.

When I first read up about my sign and saw the words "shy, sensitive, timid" used to describe characteristics of those born under my sign, I was immediately impressed. Wow, Wow, and Wow again!! Curiosity got the better of me, and I needed to know more. Delving deeper into my chart, I found out that my time of birth meant I had Saturn, the Celestial Policeman, as my ruling planet. Saturn is pretty stern, and its position in my chart explained my serious expression and skinny body.

In addition, I had my Moon in the ultra sensitive sign of Cancer—it was no wonder I was a quiet little clam! It all now made *perfect* sense to me. My more outgoing sisters were double Air signs with some Fire thrown in—a totally different astrological make-up! My youngest sister, also a double Water sign, was more like me in temperament. Yet we all came from the same genetic oven. Wonder of wonders!

I am deeply grateful for my knowledge of Astrology; to say it liberated me would be an understatement. Knowledge is power, and once I understood that my Lord and Maker had it all worked out for me, I started to accept myself. I looked in the mirror one day and said, "It is what it is. Make the best of it."

Astrology helped me to develop a much healthier relationship with myself by understanding my strengths and weaknesses. Not only that, but it helped me to understand others, too, and from this understanding came tolerance. How can we love others, if we don't understand them? And how can we understand them? Try Astrology for starters.

Each of the 12 signs is born with a purpose, and each has a role to play in making our world a better place. Each has a quality that nobody else has. Each has a talent, and each has a function. If everybody did what they were destined to do, there would be greater peace within them, and ultimately in our world.

In addition to praying to the four powerful Archangels, Michael, Gabriel, Raphael and Uriel, I would also suggest praying to your astrological angel as it helps you to realize your potential and work on your shorthcomings according to your star sign.

When I think of Aries, springtime comes to mind. Everything is fresh, new, white, and bright with possibilities. I think of little lambs dancing for joy in fields filled with hosts of golden daffodils. The air is clean, and hope is all around.

Aries is the first sign of the zodiac and, as such, is known as the "baby of the zodiac." Just like the baby, they say it like it is! Their honesty is refreshing, and their hope and resilience truly awe inspiring. No matter what life throws at them, they simply bounce back, like a baby learning to crawl—all smiles and ready to try again. They are simply irrepressible!

The three water signs (Cancer, Scorpio, Pisces) are the emotional types. They feel deeply, are highly intuitive, sensitive, and like their water element, have depth and mystery. We need them in our world to connect us to our hearts, and to each other.

The three earth signs (Taurus, Virgo, Capricorn) are the practical, down-to-earth types. Like the earth, they are solid. They are reliable, earthy, and get the job done. We need them in our world to provide stability, sensuality, and to connect us to our bodies, and reality.

As water needs earth to contain it, so too does earth need water to give it life and sustenance. Water and earth energies blend harmoniously together.

The three fire signs (Aries, Leo, Sagittarius) Fire signs are the leaders. They are courageous, energetic, adventurous, and enthusiastic. We need their dynamism, vitality, insight and initiative. We need their insight, passion, and ability to motivate.

The three air signs (Aquarius, Gemini, Libra) Air signs are the communicators of the zodiac. They are friendly, socially orientated, creative and charming. We need their imagination, intellectual inspiration, and ability to bring harmony and connection.

Just as fire needs air to fan it, so too does air need fire to make it things happen. Fire and Air energies blend harmoniously together.

ARIES (March 21 – April 20)

A Letter from your Angel to you, dear Aries:

Dear Child of Aries,

As your Guardian Angel, I love your refreshing honesty and integrity. To your own self you must always be true. Whenever you find yourself having to be less than honest, both with yourself and others, STOP! Not being true to yourself will give you a headache! Come to me in moments of turmoil and confusion. I will always be here for you.

Sure, my dear little Ram, there will be moments when you want to break free and do daring things, and go where even Angels dare to tread! Again, listen to your heart. *Think* before you act! Because Aries is ruled by the head, you can be a bit headstrong at times. Choose your battles wisely, and always trust your incredible gut instinct.

Spend some time with solid, earthy types. It's true that you may find them a tad boring on occasion, but they can teach you how to plan, strategize, be smart with your money, and follow through on your wonderful bright spark ideas. I know you don't like to be bogged down with the "small details"—you are a *big* ideas person—but a jigsaw puzzle needs all the pieces, big and small, to complete the project. Just remember that, my sweet Aries child.

You have so much potential, and are as bright and refreshing as an April flower, but impatience is a dragon you have to slay. Everything in life does not have to be so urgent! When you find yourself bursting with impatience and about to have a Martian tantrum—STOP! Take a deep breath…and talk to me! I will always be there for you.

Listen to your heart and your gut, and honour your dreams. You are the little Ram with high hopes…and I am here to help you achieve them.

Prayer to the Aries Angel:

Dear Angel of Aries,

I value your presence in my life. As the gentle Angel of nature, and my guiding light, please help me to remember the magical healing energy found in nature. When I push myself to the limit, and become exhausted and mentally drained, please refresh my spirit. Guide me back to a calm, peaceful place, where nature can restore and rejuvenate my tired mind, body, and spirit.

AMEN

TAURUS (April 21 – May 21)

A letter from your Angel to you, dear Taurus:

Dear Child of Taurus,

When I think of you, my beautiful and sensual one, I can smell the fragrant perfume of cherry blossom trees in full vibrant flower. I see the darling buds of May; I hear beautiful music; I taste delicious, aromatic food; I feel the grass beneath my feet, and the gentle caress of your finger tips. I feel the touch of soft velvet and cashmere and the sweet aroma of sandalwood. You bring love, passion, and beauty to this world.

As your Guardian Angel, I am here to help you in moments of fear and stagnation. Sometimes, as a Taurus, you don't like too much change. And you find it hard to let go—of anger, pain, and sorrow. Once you decide on a course of action, it is your way or the highway! I know you don't like when people call you stubborn, but maybe there is a tad of truth in that description!

As your Guardian Angel, I am here to protect and guide you. That stubborn, determined character you have can help you in achieving your goals, and I will help make sure they are the right goals for you! When people call you stubborn, just gift them with your beautiful Venusian smile and say, "Stubbornness is patience turned inside out!"

Yes, you are patient. You are loyal, loving, and ever so reliable. If you say you will do something, you do it! If you say you love somebody, you mean it! If somebody hurts you, you find it hard to let go of the grudge.

Pray to me, dear Taurus, and I will help you resolve inner conflicts. I will help you find peace in moments of despair. I will help you remain calm in the face of a storm. I will help you to be brave in moments of fear, and determined in moments of weakness. My gifts to you are Joy, Contentment, and Beauty.

Never forget, dear Taurus, that a thing of beauty is a joy forever! And yes, you are right, persistence if the Mother of Miracles!

Prayer to the Taurus Angel:

Dear Angel of Taurus,

I feel blessed to have you as my guiding light. In moments of anxiety, please dispel my fears. Let the warmth of your radiant love flow through me, infusing my heart with feelings of Joy, Contentment, and Peace.

When I feel fearful of making big and important changes in my life, help me to dispel my fears, and become more adaptable to change. When I become weary from working too hard, help me to relax and to connect with my body in a positive, loving way, and to be less critical of myself. When my mind becomes blocked and stagnant, help me find release.

You are the Angel of pure love—help me to open my heart to give and receive love. Let it flow through my veins like blood. Let me be a source of light, joy, consolation and comfort to all that I meet. In doing so, I represent the Divine Love with which you bless me.

AMEN

GEMINI (May 22 – June 21)

A letter from your Angel to you, dear Gemini:

Dear Child of Gemini,

When I think of you, I see a beautiful golden butterfly dancing around a garden in early summer. People are mesmerized by your beauty and agility, but when they try to catch you, you fly off far away. I see you as a dancing doll—light, charming, and ever so nimble. You are bright, vivacious, charming, chatty, and so full of life; as curious as a newborn kitten and as bubbly as a bottle of champagne. You are an eternal mystery, both to yourself and to others. As the sign of the twin, you have two sides to your nature: a light side and a dark side; a happy face and a sad one; a public self and a private self.

As your guiding Angel, I will help you when you feel blocked emotionally. I will help you to get out of your head and into your heart. I will help you to forgive others and to be more compassionate. Yes, I know you don't *mean* to hurt others. It's just that when somebody bores you and no longer holds your interest, you fly off to another more interesting person. I will help you to become more grounded and mindful, and, like a postage stamp, stick to something until you get there.

I will help you in all your communications—
pray to me for clarity, confidence, or whenever you
need assistance before a speaking engagement. I
will help calm your nerves, and be there beside
you, whispering the right words into your ear. Just
be yourself—even if it's a double act!

Prayer to the Gemini Angel:

Dear Angel of Gemini,

I am so grateful to have you as my Guardian
Angel. I pray that you will help my busy brain to
pace itself and help me to become more mindful.
Whenever I unintentionally hurt somebody, please
bring to my attention that person, and help me to
be more compassionate in my dealings. Guide
me in my personal relationships, so that I may
attract into my life people who understand me,
and know that I need a lot of mental stimulation
and emotional space.

I am sometimes so in my mind that I can
easily forget I have a body! Please help me to
connect my mind, body, and soul. Help me to
realize that despite all my wanderings, happiness
really is found within a narrow compass, and
within myself. Please ground me, calm me, and
enlighten me about my true spiritual identity.

Guide me to be a gifted communicator, so that my words, deeds, and actions will inspire and bring comfort and enlightenment to others. In doing so, I express my higher purpose and give glory to God.

AMEN

CANCER *(June 22 – July 22)*

A letter from your Angel to you, dear Cancer:

Dear Child of Cancer,

You are a daisy chain of love, connecting us all together with your sweet and caring nature. You are kindness personified: loyal, generous, and compassionate. You go about your daily life nurturing everybody you come in contact with—children, your spouse, animals, plants, the homeless and destitute—in fact, anybody who needs a helpful and caring friend knows they can rely on you to be a shoulder to cry on.

In caring for others, you sometimes are too drained and exhausted to help yourself! I am here as your Guardian Angel to help you. I know that behind your laughter and great sense of humour, there lurks a worrying streak. When you're in your "worry wart" mood, you worry about absolutely everything—mostly about money though, as I know you value your security, and try to have enough put aside for that rainy day. In times of stress, let me be the shoulder you cry on. Let me be the one to soothe your achy breaky heart. I will be your rock and your comfort. I will help you to fulfill your spiritual destiny, and to find your highest calling as a Cancerian. Pray to me when you need hope in your life, or when you have questions about the proper path to pursue. When stress and anxiety is keeping you awake at night, pray to me before you fall asleep and unburden your worries to me. I will always listen and support you. All you need do is ask and you shall receive.

Never let the clouds of worry dim the sunshine from your beautiful, caring heart.

Prayer to the Cancer Angel:

Dear Angel of Cancer,

I am blessed to have you as my Guardian Angel—your caring and gentle spirit soothes my soul. When I pray to you, I feel a sense of comfort and protection. I know that at times I worry too much, and I pray that you will please help me to worry less, and to realize that there is nothing that you and I cannot handle together.

Please help me to realize my potential in life. Help me to be a good parent to my children, and to care for all my loved ones who depend on me. Help me to be strong and resilient in the face of difficulties, and hopeful in times of sorrow and defeat.

Help me to be creative in my thoughts, words, and deeds, and to be an inspiration for others. I wish to radiate God's love by my good deeds, and in caring for others, I give glory to God who is worthy of all my love and gratitude.

AMEN

LEO *(July 23 – August 22)*

A *letter from your Angel to you, dear Leo:*

Dear Child of Leo,

You were born with the gift of leadership and have been blessed by the gods with courage, vision, dignity, and generosity of spirit. When I think of you, I envision fields full of glorious sunflowers standing tall and proud in the warm August sunshine. I feel joy, hear laughter, and see golden halos and magnificent, larger-than-life mansions. Everything is gloriously grand.

You have high standards, and I know—yes, it is true!—that your pride is something that can either work in your favour or go against you, if taken too far. Remember that old wise saying, "Pride comes before a fall," and never be afraid to admit your weaknesses, or to ask for help. I am always here for you, and I know you have a good, warm heart.

Come to me when you feel vulnerable, or when old wounds threaten to destroy your confidence. I will help heal painful memories and give you the courage you need to move forward with your life. Leave all your cares with me as you sleep, and I shall bring you the peace and contentment your soul yearns for. Remember: woe to man who relies on mere mortals! The path of your enlightenment is through spiritual growth. Your biggest critic is yourself, and your greatest ally is God; He is the only audience you shall ever need to please.

Keep your ego in check, dear Leo, and do not let it blind you to sycophants.

Just like your symbolic Leo, you were born for great things, and I am here to help you achieve them.

Prayer to the Leo Angel:

Dear Angel of Leo,

I am profoundly grateful to have you as my guiding Angel. With you, I can be my absolute self. I can be vulnerable and weak—a side of me I do not like to show the world. You know my strengths and you know my weaknesses. I want to live my life with zest, and to give of my best at all times. Whenever I become blinded by ego, and in danger of making some bad decisions in my personal or business life, please set me straight. Be the voice of reason and wisdom in my ear. Help me to attract true friends into my life who share my vision and are not afraid to dream big dreams.

I pray for your guidance to help me realize my potential as a Leo. And I pray to you for courage to stand up for what I believe in. I want to live my life with purpose, intention, and integrity. Help me to release any limiting beliefs and fears that may stand in my way. You alone know the secrets of the universe as given to you by God. Please guide me on my spiritual journey and help me to open my mind and heart to receive, so that by my noble deeds, I become worthy of God's love, and a living example of what it means to be a true follower of Christ.

AMEN

VIRGO *(August 23 – September 22)*

A letter from your Angel to you, dear Virgo:

Dear Child of Virgo,

When I think of you, I see busy little bees making honey and armies of ants going about their business in a practical, hard-working manner. I see fields of calming lavender and neat rows of ocean blue cornflowers. I can smell the pure fragrance of lily of the valley and newly laundered sheets. I see a beautiful, gentle spirit, who more than anything else wants to be useful and kind.

I see doctors, nurses, veterinarians, teachers, writers, and people dedicated to their work and families. I see animals being lovingly cared for. I see peace, but I also see a lot of self-criticism, anxiety, and fretting over things that may never ever happen. Yes, you can be a worrywart, dear Virgo, and that is why I am here to help you, just like you help others. I want to help you heal yourself when worries and anxiety threaten to weaken your resolve and cause ill health. I want to help you build up your self-confidence in moments of self-doubt. I will help you to relax and follow your true calling. Come to me when you feel overwhelmed with responsibility and stress. I am here to help you—all you need to do is ask.

Just remember, dear Virgo, you must pace yourself, and find a balance in your life between work and play. Let me be your spiritual coach!

Prayer to the Virgo Angel

Dear Angel of Virgo,

I am very grateful to have you as my guiding Angel. In moments of anxiety and worry, please help me to stay calm and grounded. I know that at times I get so caught up in my work, and my desire to feel useful, that I forget I need to have moments of rest, too! Help me to relax and increase my self-confidence in moments of self-doubt. Please be my guide and counselor on my spiritual journey, so that my faith becomes my rock, and a source of consolation to others.

I pray that you will help me find my true vocation, and that my life will be a happy and productive one, blessed with good health, a kind, supportive spouse, healthy and happy children, and the opportunity to give glory to God through my actions, words, and deeds. Lastly, I pray for all the vulnerable in our society: animals, homeless people, and victims of war and violence. Please guide, protect, and help them.

AMEN

LIBRA *(September 22 – October 22)*

A *letter from your Angel to you, dear Libra:*

Dear Child of Libra,

When I think of you, I see your beautiful, radiant smile that lights up any room. I see harmony, elegance, and charisma. I see images of peace and love; I hear sweet, beautiful music. Pleasure, fine wine, and conversation are flowing with ease. Everybody is having fun, and you are delighted, because happy people make you happy—right? Peace and Harmony are your middle names. That's what I am all about, too, so when you find your life is in disarray, just call on me, dear child: I'm here for you. In me, you will find the peace you are looking for.

In your perfect world, everything would be fair and just, and there would be no wars (just like Libran John Lennon sang about all those years ago). You were born to bring beauty to this world, dear Libra, and to connect people in perfect harmony. You are a connector, a singer, a designer, and a creator of art in all its forms: clothes, music, interiors, fabrics, flowers, make-up… Wherever beauty and harmony is needed, you deliver 100% because you give it your all!

When the world does not give you what you are looking for, dear Libra, or you become unbalanced by disharmony around you, find yourself a beautiful little prayer altar, be it in your garden, your home, or your heart. Play soft, soothing music, centre yourself through relaxation exercises, and spend some time with me. Together we'll set the world right again!

Prayer to the Libra Angel

Dear Angel of Libra,

I wish the world was always at peace. I just cannot stand disharmony—it really bothers me. I want people to get along, to not say means things to each other, and to just try to accept each other. We are all different yet come from the same source of Divine love and creation. God loves us all, so why can we not do the same for each other?

Life is like a weighing scale, and there has to be balance for the scales of justice to do their thing. Please help me to find the balance in my life that I so desperately seek. I want my life to be one of beauty and harmony. Doing creative things makes me happy, because I know that by bringing beauty to others, I have the ability to make them smile, expand their world, and let them see the possibilities all around.

When I am not happy on the inside, the creativity dries up. In moments such as this, dear Libra Angel, please be my rock of calm and my oasis in a desert of disharmony so that I can do what God created me to do, and bring pleasure and beauty to the world. All we need is love, and if I have that in my life, then it will anchor me and I can radiate the love of God from within me to each and every person that I encounter.

AMEN

SCORPIO (*October 23 – November 21*)

A letter from your Angel to you, dear Scorpio:

Dear Child of Scorpio,

You are the strong and silent type, but sometimes this can go against you, especially when you allow hurts and resentments to bottle up inside your sensitive little soul. You were born for greater things. God has blessed you with stamina, determination, and tremendous energy. When I think of you, I see beautiful and sometimes sad eyes, powerful perception, great intelligence, a loyal and loving nature, and someone who is determined to make the world a better place.

I am glad to be your protective Angel, as I think we will be able to form a tight and supportive friendship. I know you have a good heart, and can be very caring and loyal to those that you love. I truly want you to be happy and at peace with yourself. I will encourage you to express your deepest feelings and to not be afraid to keep things out in the open. I will encourage you to perform random acts of kindness, and to live your life as God would want you to. I will help you to create a healthy balance between work and play, and to be so confident in yourself that any traits of jealousy and possessiveness on your part will disappear. I am here for you always as your confidante, spiritual advisor, and, most importantly, your friend. Whatever you ask of me in prayer shall be granted, if it is the will of God.

Prayer to the Scorpio Angel:

Dear Angel of Scorpio,

I am deeply grateful to God for making you a powerful channel through which he can communicate with me. Whatever wrongs I may have committed in my life, please help me to make amends. Guide me on the right path that will fill my heart with joy, contentment, and peace.

Please help me to realize my potential as a Scorpio. I know God has a plan for me, and I pray that he will make it known to me so that I can make a valuable contribution to society, and be a genuine inspiration to others. Please help me to be more open and trusting of others. When I have been hurt by someone, grant me the courage to let the offender know and to move on without letting it fester within me.

Help me to deepen my faith, and to grow so strong in my love for God, that all the trials and tribulations of life no longer leave a dent in my heart.

I pray to you, dear Scorpio Angel, to guide me in my thoughts, words, and deeds, so that everything I say or do gives glory to God, who is deserving of all my love.

AMEN

SAGITTARIUS (*November 22 – December 21*)

A letter from your Angel to you, dear Sagittarius:

Hey Buddy!

I'm here for you. Like it or not, we're a team—and a dream team at that! I share your generous and friendly spirit and want to help you on your exciting spiritual journey. I know you are a big and deep thinker; you are a seeker of knowledge and truth, and are on an endless quest to discover the meaning of life. I'm here to help provide the answers to many of your questions. Pray to me for guidance, as I truly want you to realize your vast potential as a Sagittarius.

You were born for great things! If you find yourself procrastinating, eating too much, or gambling excessively, pray to me for guidance, and I will help keep you on track, and manage both your weight and your money. I know you were born under Jupiter, the largest planet in the solar system, but hey! That doesn't mean you should promise more than you can realistically deliver, or eat more than you should, or gamble like there is no tomorrow. Boundaries, my dear Sagittarius!

You like to say it like it is and cut to the chase, am I right? But if your outspoken nature verges on the overly sharp and your words cut like a knife, then just have a chat with me. I will help you soften your words!

Like I said dear Sagittarius, I'm here for you 24/7. Just dial H for Heaven!

Patricia O'Neill

Prayer to the Sagittarius Angel

Dear Angel of Sagittarius,

Thank you for being there for me. I know sometimes I like to run with life, throw caution to the wind, speak without thinking, and live my life with occasional "reckless abandon," so I really appreciate your help in reining me in. Just like a bolting horse, I need that harness! I appreciate the fact you understand my nature, and know I do need space to grow and think, yet at the same time can be the beneficiary of balance and harmony in my life. There is always a need for peace within.

I'm very glad to have you as my spiritual guide, and would appreciate your help in developing and strengthening my faith. Finally, I call upon you, dear Sagittarius Angel, to infuse me with discipline, balance, and order in my life, so that I can give of my best, and not offend others with my words but rather inspire them! I want to do great things, and with your help I will! I want to be a beacon of light leading others to God—by my example and good works.

AMEN

CAPRICORN *(December 22 – January 20)*

A letter from your Angel to you, dear Capricorn:

Dear Child of Capricorn,

You came into the world an "old soul" with the responsibilities of the world on your tiny little shoulders (or so it seemed at times!). You know how it feels to suffer, worry, and bear responsibility. Born under the stern planet of Saturn, you learned from a very young age that life is not always easy— or fair, for that matter! But against that, dear one, you were born with grit, determination, a strong work ethic, high standards, and an appetite for success. You just need to remember that all work and no play makes for a limited life; you must balance the rough with the smooth.

When the cares of life become too much, come to me in prayer. I will help you connect with your feelings and emotions. I will help you heal past pain, anger, and grief, so that you can move on with your life without the burden of heavy emotional baggage! Just remember, dear one, I am here for you always. I will help you realize all your potential, minus the pain.

Patricia O'Neill

Prayer to the Capricorn Angel

Dear Angel of Capricorn,

There are times in my life when I worry and fret about the future. Life can be so difficult, and sometimes it feels as if I am constantly struggling against the tide. I work very hard, and yet challenges come up to bite me on a regular basis. Is it me? Or is it just life? I need your help to keep me buoyant and positive. I know you are the Angel of Transition and Change, so please help me ride the dark waves of depression when they threaten to drown me in sorrow.

Some days I feel fine, other days not so. On the not-so-sunny days, please be my guide and comfort. Please help me to see the sunshine beyond the clouds. I have a funny side, and I have a fighting spirit, so I know that with your help, there is nothing I cannot achieve in my life. I pray for good health, stamina, positive ideation, and the ability to give back to the world, and make a worthy contribution.

AMEN

AQUARIUS (*January 21 – February 19*)

A *letter from your Angel to you, dear Aquarius:*

Dear Child of Aquarius,

You try to be all things to all men, and get worn out in the process! Don't spread yourself too thin, dear one, or your nerves will become frazzled and you'll end up positively exhausted! Friends are good, but too many can make you become scattered. It is wise for you to take a deep breath before you enter the day, meditate, and set your intentions in a calm, mindful, way. As the bringer of knowledge, I can help you to visualize your vast potential as an Aquarius—and it is indeed vast!

Whenever you find yourself lost or confused in your life, I will guide and assist you along the way, helping you to visualize your future. I will teach you how to live each day with gratitude and appreciation, so that your life becomes richer, and closer to the Divine Plan set out for you at birth. I will teach you about friendship, so that only true friends will come into your life.

I will help you to tap into your inner power, and increase your creativity, so that your mind will become open to receiving messages from the Divine. Your task in this life is to bring innovative ideas, intelligence, wisdom, compassion, and understanding to others. I will help you in your mission. All you need to do is ask!

Prayer to the Aquarius Angel

Dear Angel of Aquarius,

Please help me whenever I spread myself too thin, and my nerves become rattled. Be my guide in the dark moments of confusion and my anchor and my strength when I lose my way. Please help me to keep my busy wits about me, and to remain grounded and calm, especially in moments when I feel anything but calm! I want to be a good friend to others, and I would love to have good friends in my life, too. Please help me to choose my friends wisely, so that we will be a blessing for each other on life's journey.

I call upon your vision to help me realize my purpose and potential in life.

I want to be a source of wisdom and inspiration to everyone I meet. Please inspire me to think great thoughts, and create innovative ideas for others, so that I too can be an Angel of light along life's dark pathway.

Help me to love what is worth loving in this life, and to value what is precious in the eyes of God. Bestow upon me good health, strength, and inspiration to carry out the work He wants me to do. Grant that I may always do, and give, all that I can, to make life easy for those in need. For this I pray.

AMEN

PISCES (February 20 – March 20)

A letter from your Angel to you, dear Pisces:

Dear Child of Pisces,

You have much to contribute to this world. When I tune into your mystical vibes, I hear beautiful music, see exquisite art and mesmerizing dance, and experience heart-warming kindness and compassion. You have empathy, understanding, and the wisdom of the Universe at your fingertips. As the twelfth and last sign of the zodiac, you have walked in the shoes of all the eleven signs preceding you, which is why you are known as the "wise one." You see more than others see, and you feel more than others feel. "Still waters run deep" is a phrase that springs to mind when describing you because you are deeper than the deepest ocean.

With all that talent, dear one, there are many paths you can follow. Sometimes I know you get confused and don't know how to focus your attention, or in which direction you should go. I will help you find motivation and focus. I will help you manifest your dreams into reality. I will help you find inner peace by following your heart. I will show you the way.

Call on me to be your friend and ally. I know what is in your heart and will help you achieve your dearest dreams. Believe in me as I believe in you. Trust in me, pray to me, walk with me in gardens and forests. Love me through animals and vulnerable ones. In being kind to others, you are being kind to me.

I will connect with you through music and words. Be receptive to meaningful lyrics, as that is how I will communicate with you. If you find yourself experiencing a creative block, I will help open the sluice gates of your imagination, so the music and magic will flow. Trust in me, dear Pisces, and let the love between us flow. I am here for you always. Seek and you shall find. Pray and your prayers shall be answered.

Prayer to the Angel of Pisces

Dear Angel of Pisces,

I am very lucky to have you as my guide. God could not have chosen a more perfect match for me! I love your kindness and understanding, as well as your practical side. Sometimes I get very confused, and I don't know which path to pursue. In moments such as these, please steer me in the right direction. Help me to realize my potential as a Pisces. Guide, discipline, focus, and motivate me in moments of weakness and inertia.

Please help me to manifest my dreams, and to find people who can help me realize those dreams. I pray for good luck in my endeavours, and that when my work is done to the best of my ability, I will be in the right place at the right time! I trust in you absolutely and completely.

When the waters of my imagination dry up, please help the flow of creativity to return once again. Inspire me to create work that will gladden the hearts of many. Finally, dear Pisces Angel, please help me to be a source of joy, comfort, and love to those less fortunate. Give me ways to show my gratitude to God; not just in words, but by my actions. For this I pray.

AMEN